A S H
+ SALT

Sarah Grace is a solicitor and certified yoga teacher. Of French and Irish nationality, raised in Japan and France, she obtained an LLB degree in law and French law from University College London and Université Paris II Panthéon-Assas.

After surviving a violent sexual assault in 2019 that turned her life upside down, Sarah publicly called for changes to Ireland's criminal justice system for other sexual violence survivors, which culminated in her meeting with Minister for Justice Helen McEntee TD and the Office of the Director of Public Prosecutions (DPP) in March 2021 to discuss legal reforms.

Through her Instagram account, @busywarrioryoga, she shares motivational content, tips on healing, and yoga tutorials.

In recognition of her work and of the remarkable difference she made in Irish society, Sarah was awarded the *Irish Tatler* Women of the Year Special Recognition Award in 2021.

ASH + SALT

FROM SURVIVAL TO EMPOWERMENT
AFTER SEXUAL ASSAULT

Sarah Grace

THE O'BRIEN PRESS
DUBLIN

First published 2022 by The O'Brien Press Ltd,
12 Terenure Road East, Rathgar, Dublin 6, D06 HD27, Ireland.
Tel: +353 1 4923333; Fax: +353 1 4922777
E-mail: books@obrien.ie Website: obrien.ie
The O'Brien Press is a member of Publishing Ireland.

ISBN: 978-1-78849-316-1
Text © Sarah Grace 2022
The moral rights of the author have been asserted.
Editing, typesetting, layout, design © The O'Brien Press Ltd

Author photograph (back cover and p 2) by Alison Grace.
Cover and internal design by Emma Byrne.

8 7 6 5 4 3 2 1
25 24 23 22

Printed and bound by Scandbook AB, Sweden.
The paper in this book is produced using pulp from managed forests.

Published in

DUBLIN

UNESCO
City of Literature

Dedication

For Alison, who carried me through it all and whose courage
roared when the last of mine died out.
To Dad and *Maman*, for always guiding me to rise above
and to choose love over hate.
To Erika, Kunak and Eileen, for never letting me
forget what kickass women can achieve.

Contents

Introduction

When we hear the word warrior, our minds instinctively travel to the stories of mythical heroes and demigods, of epic battles and brandished swords glinting in the snow, of rallying war cries echoing through the fields as the first rays of dawn break across the horizon. We forget that there are warriors much closer to home, fighting invisible battles every day.

The purpose of this book is to shed light on what sexual violence survivors go through, both on their path to recovery and in the challenges they face within the criminal justice system. The aim is to encourage a wider dialogue around sexual assault, but also to provide a first-hand account to guide survivors and their loved ones through the process ahead. This book is for everyone, not just survivors, not just women. Sexual assault affects all of us. It impacts women, men and people, as well as their friends, families, partners and colleagues. It is just as much a man's issue as it is a woman's plight, not only because men are survivors too but also because it is going to take everyone's voice to tackle this beast. If a community is afraid to talk openly about sexual violence or rape culture, it cannot protect its people by calling out the behaviours that allow those things to thrive. The reason sexual assault cuts so deeply into us as a society is because we have never been taught how to address such things, despite them often happening under our very noses. There is an expectation that we do not speak about such unpalatable things in polite society, and so we do not know what to do or how to behave around survivors.

That lack of speaking up is devastating. Passing through such life-altering trauma is already the most isolating thing in the world because so few can relate, but the collective silence on the issue pushes survivors even deeper into the shadows. People are afraid to meet our gaze, friends fall away, and feelings of shame and guilt set in that make us feel completely alone in the crowd. I chose to break my silence by sharing my story publicly. That is what it will take to force change. And yet, the heavy weight of societal judgement and the high cost of the privacy you must give up in order to speak out means that for many survivors it is a near-impossible sacrifice to make.

The critical importance of breaking down the taboo around sexual assault becomes even clearer when you consider the sheer number of survivors. A 2020 study led by Trinity College Dublin and NUI Maynooth found that 15% of Irish adults have been raped at some point in their lifetime and one-third have experienced some form of sexual violence. In 2002, when the last SAVI (Sexual Abuse and Violence in Ireland) report was compiled, that figure stood at 25% of Irish men and 42% of Irish women having experienced sexual violence. We have made no progress in twenty years.

Survivors are up against the likes of post-traumatic stress disorder (PTSD), the social stigma around sexual assault, and a court system that is heavily loaded against them. They must face such Titans, often without any arms or ammunition. I was privileged in that department. I had a range of defences at my disposal that many do not. As a lawyer, I had nuggets of invaluable knowledge on legal procedure and criminal investigations. As a yoga teacher, I was trained in mental resilience and possessed the tools to tap into my self-awareness and kindle my healing. I was also lucky enough to have my incredible family there to support me every step of the way. By contrast, more than half of survivors in Ireland don't tell anyone. There are warriors out there who every day are taking on the toughest fight of their lives, alone. I cannot imagine how any person could do it without that support, and to all of you who have walked this path before me, no matter your journey and outcome, you are my heroes.

And yet, despite all these advantages that I had, steering through PTSD and our impossibly convoluted criminal justice system was the hardest thing I have ever had to do. Although I was the victim of unspeakable trauma, at many points I felt I was the one on trial. From day one after my assault, I realised just how little I knew about how to survive something like this, and it came very close to breaking me. So now, I want to arm you with every weapon and shield in my arsenal because, make no mistake, you are not walking into a fair fight. This book is your survival guide. I am writing to you as I would to a friend, to equip you with the tools you'll need to help you navigate the tricky path ahead, whether it's on your own journey or helping a survivor.

But this book alone is not enough. The Irish justice system is broken, and one warrior alone cannot take on an entire institution. Warriors need armies, and this is where you, the people, come in. This is a call to arms. A peaceful one, mind you, but we need your voice to amplify those that are muted.

To all of you who have not walked through the fire of sexual violence, this is your fight too. You wield great power, perhaps unbeknownst to you, to make change happen. Our laws and systems reflect the values and standards we aspire to as a society. They reflect who we are as a people. Anything short of treating all parties with humanity and respect, both the survivor and the accused, should be strongly rejected by all of us. We all have a responsibility to push for change and to hold our elected representatives accountable.

People with influence, people in the political and judicial spheres, educators, policy-makers, managers, legal practitioners, it falls on you most of all to take up this responsibility and speak up about sexual violence, about mental health, safety, acceptance and inclusion.

The reforms contemplated here are not difficult. This is not asking for the seas to be parted. We are not asking for the perfect system, or a colossal overhaul of our judicial and social networks. All we are asking for is a little empathy in how we treat survivors, and the scrapping of some antiquated legal provisions that have no place in our modern laws. Ireland has blazed a trail forward in recent years in fighting for fairer and more progressive laws. We were the first nation to legalise marriage equality by popular vote, we have torn down outdated laws on divorce and abortion. I have every faith that this will be yet another area in which we can lead the way and be proud of what our nation can achieve.

I should note that aside from my wonderful family, all names and personal details cited have been changed to protect people's identities. This is an honest account of what happened to me and the learnings I want to share. The views expressed in this book are mine alone. I am not a medical expert. I cannot speak to any other experience than my own. I speak to you only as a survivor. But throughout my journey I was given helpful insights from other survivors, from therapists, lawyers, experts and heads of organisations and government departments, which are threaded through my own observations and experiences.

This a book written for Ireland, but also for everywhere else in the world, because we still have a long way to go to shatter the stigma of sexual violence and to tear down the barriers preventing survivors from obtaining justice. This is my story, but it is also the story of every survivor who honoured me by sharing theirs with me. This is about sexual assault, but it is also about healing from deep-rooted trauma and finding your way back to compassion and acceptance.

Ultimately, my message is one of hope. To the survivors and their families and friends, I hope you know that you are not alone in this, and that none of this was your fault. Whatever your story is, what I want you to take away from this book is that you are capable of wondrous things. Your recovery is within reach, and it is a life-changing opportunity for transformation, if you embrace it. As daunted as you may feel, know that you will come out of this stronger, kinder, more complex and with a deeper lust for life than you could imagine. You can come to love this healing journey of yours, because through the pain and the heartbreak and the loss, you will become whole.

Your healing is a beautiful thing, and it will shine like a beacon of light for others in their time of darkness.

1.

Fight, Flight, Freeze or Fawn: The Assault

17 July 2019
'This can't be happening.'

My story starts in Connemara. It's a surprisingly warm evening, even for July, and I'm watching the most mesmerising sunset against a backdrop of a long, white beach strewn with dramatic black rocks and archipelagos. The shimmering light is dancing across the water, streaks of fuchsia, golden amber and blazing tangerine. Movie stuff.

We've rented this jewel of an Airbnb, tucked away in the zig-zagging coastline between Glassilaun beach and Killary bay. My parents and my sister, Alison, are here, preparing dinner and chatting away in the background. The house is perched at the top of a cliff and the garden slopes all the way down to the pearly white beach below. Since we arrived, I've sat here every morning with my steaming cup of coffee and every evening to watch the sun take itself to bed. The view does not get old. Now I'm sipping a glass of champagne, I've lost count of the number exactly, taking stock.

I've been living in Ireland for over three years now. I moved here from my home in France in 2016 to train as a solicitor in a law firm based in Dublin's financial hub. To be perfectly honest, the start was a little rough and Ireland took some acclimatising to. Having travelled all over the place – raised in Japan and France by a French mother and an Irish father, studied at university in London, following which I travelled for a year around Spain and Cambodia – Dublin was a wee bit of a culture shock at first. I struggled with the cold weather, the lack of diversity compared to London, even the culture at times (I mean, Irish wakes still beat the *hell* outta me). But I've come a long way since then. I've made amazing friends, built a life for myself here. I qualified as a yoga teacher two years ago and, finally, *finally*, as a lawyer seven months ago. I'm looking at this spectacular beach, surrounded by my family, on a cheeky long weekend away in the west of Ireland after my parchment ceremony at the Law Society (they actually do present you with a parchment roll – Hogwarts got nothing on us) and the two days of drinking ourselves stupid that followed. Life is good.

I take another sip. Tastes like victory to me. Being a yoga teacher, I'm all about humility and letting things go, but screw it, sometimes you have to allow yourself a little moment to indulge. It's all about balance, right? I'm due back in work tomorrow, but it's a lazy afternoon and I've taken the executive decision to stay here an extra night and get the early train back to Dublin tomorrow, rather than travel back tonight. I'm feeling extra smug that evening, no Sunday fear in sight.

This was a brilliant idea.

* * *

The alarm goes off at 4.50am, shrieking like a tone-deaf banshee.

This was a terrible idea.

I get up gingerly, stumble to the bathroom and slap some cold water on my face. *Am I getting old or has my skin always felt this dry?* My eyes are sore. Making my way to the kitchen, I find that Dad and Alison are up, too, and far too chirpy for this early in the morning. They're like two little morning birds, light-footed and sprightly. I grumble to myself, *must be nice not to have a work week looming ahead.* We grab our coats and my bag and bundle ourselves into the car.

The hour-long drive to Galway is smooth, in reverent silence for the dawn sky, which is glowing brighter by the minute. There's the occasional heavy shower, rain droplets bigger than hailstones dramatically lashing themselves onto the windscreen, and then the heavens clear again. It's just us and the rocky hills, no one is on the road. Good Lord, Ireland really is beautiful sometimes. I'm taking stock again.

* * *

I catch some interrupted sleep on the train before it pulls into Dublin, and then from Heuston Station it's straight to the office, no time to swing home first. I drop the suitcase by my desk and hastily make my way up to the showers to get changed.

Friends stop by my office to say hello.

'How was Connemara?'

I grin. 'Amazing.'

'I'm still recovering from the three-day piss-up that followed Thursday.'

'Same, very glad I had a few days' R&R in Connemara.'

My grin quickly dissipates when I see the towering bundle of documents on my chair.

'Is that all for me?'

No rest for the wicked.

It's a full day of back-to-back meetings and catching up on work. It would honestly persuade you against ever taking any holidays when you get back to the work that's piled up in your absence. We have two important meetings tomorrow and I've been asked to lead the corporate side. (*Me!*) The first is with this cool new tech client considering a potential invest-ment into an exciting green technology project. I can already picture the glowing headlines in the newspapers. The second meeting is with royalty, apparently.

'Royalty?' I'd asked. 'Didn't we have a big uprising here about not having that?'

'Well, as close as you can get to royalty in Ireland,' was the response.

No idea what that means, but it sounds equally career-launching to me.

It's a late night in the office getting everything ready for the royals. I'm doing over questions in my head while preparing the briefs. (*Do I curtsy? Does one shake royalty's hand? Do I wear a trendy blazer or a Downton Abbey-esque suit?*) I'm practically skipping on my way home despite the tiredness.

It's stifling hot in my room when I get home. Man, these apartments can really hold humidity. I live with two friends, for this book we'll call them Niamh and Ashleigh, and our apartment is on the canal so there's just no escaping the dampness. The room has been unventilated since I left for the long weekend, so I pop open the window on the safety latch. A quick dinner and decadently steaming shower later and the air in the room is still muggy from the summer heat. We had been told by the housing agency when we first moved in that the safety latches were perfectly secure as long as we were in the apartment. The issue, we were told, was if we left the place unsupervised for a few days, as no one would hear the loud noise if someone were to force entry. I check the safety latch again and give the window a good shake. It holds steady. *Grand.* I hop into bed and soon slip into exquisite unconsciousness from all the exhaustion, questions about curtsies and outfits still milling around in my head.

TRIGGER WARNING! I'm going to pause here, dear reader, and sign-post this next part. This next passage contains a description of a violent sexual assault, so if you're worried that it might trigger you, skip on head to the next signpost (page 26). I'll meet you there.

I wake up suddenly, in the middle of the night. I often get quite bad insomnia, so it isn't uncommon for me to wake in the early hours of the morning, but something that night feels different. Normally, the amber glow from the streetlamp outside my window streams into my bedroom through the sides of the blackout curtains, but my eyes are open and it's still pitch black.

I groggily try to sit up, but something is preventing me from moving. There is a weight on my chest. I try to sit up again. Nothing.

Maybe I'm having sleep paralysis? Friends have told me stories of waking up and being unable to move or open their eyes for minutes on end, which had always fascinated me.

Hang on a second, my eyes are open. I notice the air I'm breathing is hot and humid, like a panting dog's breath. And then the smell hits me. The stench of stale cigarettes mingled with sweat and body odour fills my nostrils. I feel something slimy lick my neck.

Something is seriously wrong.

I try to sit up a third time, more forcefully now. Slowly, the shadow that had been stooped over my eyes, blocking the light from the streetlamp outside, pulls back, and I see the silhouette of a man drawn against the amber light.

It is insane the number of far-fetched scenarios your brain will go through in nanoseconds before it finally reaches the awful conclusion. My first thought when I initially woke up was that maybe I had been woken by my parents to go for our usual early morning walk. But then I remember that I'm not in Connemara anymore. I'm back in my room in Dublin. For the next split second, I thought the licking maybe came from a dog, but then quickly dismissed this thought. *We don't have a dog*, I remembered wisely. *Maybe it's my boyfriend waking me up for some early morning delight?* I racked my brain. Nope, definitely still single last time I checked. In fact, no man lives in the apartment.

It's dark in the bedroom, but with the help of the streetlight I can now make out the outline of the man's face. I do not know him. He has dark stubble, and a baseball cap shadows parts of his face.

Maybe I came home at lunchtime to let the electrician in because of some issue I can't remember, and then maybe I fainted and now he's just trying to wake me up?

Those few seconds trying to make sense of the situation seem to drag on for minutes. After every other possible scenario has run through my mind, I eventually arrive at the stomach-dropping realisation: there is a complete stranger on top of me right now.

'*What's happening?!*'

Even I am surprised at the amount of panic in my voice.

The man shushes me. He actually *shushes* me, like someone trying to comfort a young child frightened by a nightmare – the audacity. Maybe he thought he was having a romantic moment with some woman he just happened to climb on top of while burgling her house in the middle of the night, who the hell knows.

Where did he even get in from?

He leans forward, pushing me back down on the bed.

'WHAT'S HAPPENING?!'

Hands close around my throat. He begins strangling me.

This can't be happening.

I weave my hands between his arms, desperately trying to push him aside. Surely I am having a nightmare? It has to be like something out of that scene in *50 First Dates* where Lucy wakes up and has forgotten the stranger sleeping next to her is actually her lover. I'm going to wake up in a second and we'll all be laughing about this over breakfast. I keep flailing, waiting for the moment when my eyes fly open and I wake up from this nightmare. It never comes.

Fighting him off for what must have been seconds lapses into what feels like a lifetime. I grab his clenched hands to loosen his grip, wrenching them away from my throat. He slams my wrists down onto the bed. Frantically, I twist them out of his grasp to push him away, and the sickening cycle starts again, like a perverse merry-go-round. The stench of cigarettes and body odour is overpowering. I try to kick him off, but my legs are pinned down by the bedsheets which (thankfully) still separate him from me. Bucking and thrashing, alarm bells are sounding in my head, deafening.

Get him OFF!

He seems surprised that I'm resisting so much as I am able to dislodge him quickly enough. I throw him off the bed, sending the blankets sailing along after him. He goes tumbling to the right, and I leap out to the left of the bed and break into a sprint towards the door. Before I can reach it, a pair of hands grabs me from behind and I'm tackled to the ground. I land face down – hard – and whip around as I know what's coming.

He comes bearing down on top of me and starts strangling me again, harder this time. He has me straddled under his weight, my back to the floor, so there is no way out. I scream again, thinking by now surely the neighbours upstairs will have heard the commotion, surely my flatmates will be rushing to help me? No one comes. He leans forward and starts pressing his entire body weight down on my throat.

This cannot be happening. This only happens in movies. This actually cannot be happening.

I can't breathe. I can't scream.

I am going to die.

Gasping for air, with my neck pinned to the ground, I can see my bedroom behind my attacker from the corner of my eye. In that moment it hits me that this is the last thing I'm ever going to see. This is where my parents will come in, traumatised out of their lives, trying to imagine their daughter's last moments and what could have been going through her mind. *My parents are going to have to come into this room and clear out my things because I am going to be dead.* The last lucid thought that goes through my mind is the image of them holding each other, unable to leave this room as their shoulders rock from the never-ending waves of grief. And then the adrenaline kicks in.

Over. My. Dead. Body.

Adrenaline is a wondrous thing. That's one thing the movies do get right

– time really does magically slow down. Every second you have feels like three. I know now that no one is coming to save me. If I don't get myself out, he is going to kill me. It's me or him, so I need to kill *him*.

Before I could even form the thought properly, my hands have already shot up between his arms and grabbed hold of his neck. I grip my attacker as hard as I can and begin choking him back. (*Aha! The strangler becomes the stranglee!*) Despite being in the dark, I sense the clear shock register on his face. He completely lets go of my throat, instinctively reaching back to protect his own. Before he can, I slide my hands up to grip the sides of his face and try shoving my thumbs into his eyes. He screeches and sits further back, to get beyond my reach. And there is my opening – his core is exposed.

Punch him in the stomach.

Before I can register that my back is to the floor and I don't have room to take the punch, my hand has already moved down to his next weak spot and closed around his crotch. The fabric he's wearing down there is disturbingly thin. No matter.

Do not blow this shot, this is your last chance to escape.

With as much strength as I can muster I tighten my grip, crushing down on his delicates before I twist violently and yank downwards. He makes a sound I did not know a human could make and falls to the side. I kick out at him for good measure and hear a satisfying yelp.

Before I can get up off the floor, he comes bearing down a third time and wrestles me back down. The whites of his eyes, wide with rage, cut through the darkness of the room, his face pulled back into an animalistic snarl.

You blew it. You had one chance and it's gone. And now you're going to die.

I try to scream out again, in complete panic and despair.

Surely I have woken up half of Dublin by now? Why the hell is no one coming?!

He slams his hand down over my mouth to stop the screaming, his palm spread so wide it is blocking my nose as well. I can't breathe at all now.

Well, you've got nothing left to lose now.

Jerking my head to the side, I'm able to free my upper lip for a second – and a second is all I need. My teeth close around the piece of skin between his thumb and index finger.

Got you, you little shit.

I bite down, hard, and do not stop until I feel my teeth come into contact with each other and rip out a piece of flesh. He screams and collapses to the right. The foreign object is in my mouth, tasting of cold tobacco and dry as the skin of a drum. I spit it out in its ex-owner's direction (in hindsight, an extremely satisfying memory), and scramble to my feet. The door is mere feet away. I lunge forward.

The next thing I register as I take that first lunge is a sharp pain erupting inside me, radiating through my core.

I've been stabbed.

I do not stop. I do not break my run. It is only when I reach the door that I register what has happened.

That was his fingers.

He rammed them up inside me with such a force that his fingernail left an internal cut tracing the entire length of the blow. The ultimate 'fuck you' act, literally.

Fine, I thought, *if this is the price I have to pay to make it out alive, so be it.*

I slam down on the door handle and wrench it back with the full weight of my body. It does not budge.

NO!

I wrestle with it desperately. It's locked. My stomach drops.

That's it, I'm dead now. No way I'm getting a third chance to escape.

I whip around to face my attacker and am met with the most joyous of sights. He is running away!

Not stopping to ask questions, I spin back around and quickly fumble with the bolt before prising the door open. Slamming it shut behind me, I hesitate for a split second while deciding where to run. I know my two flatmates also sleep with their doors locked. Just in case an intruder comes in at night, I think bitterly. There are knives in the kitchen, but I might not make the run if he comes after me. Clutching the door handle in place, I ram my shoulder up against it to prevent him from opening it. I have no idea if he is running away to get a weapon, or even an accomplice. Screaming my flatmates' names for dear life, the pain is still throbbing inside me when Niamh's light flicks on, shining through the door frame. A muffled 'I'm coming' comes out of one of the rooms.

'Please hurry, he's still here!'

'Fuck. I'm coming, I'm coming!'

The intruder hasn't tried the bedroom door yet, but I am expecting it to start forcing down on my shoulder at any second. Ashleigh's door flies open. I take a deep breath and release my door, bolting in through hers. We hurl the door shut but as it closes, we feel it kick back. *He's coming after us.* Ramming ourselves against the door to fend him off, we look down to see what is blocking the door and realise it isn't the intruder, it's Ashleigh's blanket! It got caught in the door as she jumped out of bed. I whip it back and she slams the door shut.

'Lock the door!'

There is a moment's complete stillness as we stare at each other, eyes wide with shock.

'There was a man in my room. He attacked me.' My breathing is laboured.

A million questions are running across Ashleigh's face. I can read them from where I'm standing – *How did this happen? Where did he come from? Who is he? Is he still here? Are there others?*

In answer to all of these, the words tumble out of my mouth. 'He rammed his fingers inside me.'

Her eyes widen even more in horror. She gasps softly. 'What…?' I see the emotion rise in her eyes, and then stop in its tracks as action mode kicks in. She grabs her phone. 'We need to call for help.'

TRIGGER WARNING ENDS – Welcome back! Take a deep breath, we're OK from here onwards.

As Ashleigh places the call to the guards,[1] I pace up and down the room frantically.

'I don't know where he went. I don't know if he's coming back, or if he has back-up … or a weapon? What do we do?'

Ashleigh hangs up the call. 'They're on their way.'

'What if he comes back?' I say, panicking. 'We're not safe waiting here if he comes back.'

'We need to get out of here.'

'What about Niamh?'

'I'll call her.' Ashleigh puts the phone back to her ear. 'It's not picking up.'

We listen in dead silence for a sound.

---

1 For my non-Irish readers, you'll hear the term 'garda' a lot in this book. An Garda Síochána is the national police force in Ireland. An individual officer is referred to as a garda, and the plural is gardaí. They are also colloquially referred to as 'guards'.

'I saw her light come on when I was in the hallway.'

We listen again. Nothing.

'We need to go, Sarah.'

'What time is it?'

She checks her phone.

'Three-thirty am.'

'We need to hide somewhere safe. It's Tuesday night, there's nowhere for five blocks that'll be open right now.' I pause. 'What about a taxi? We can wait in there while the guards arrive.'

'I'll Hailo one.' She taps at her app.

'Yes, good idea.' I look down at my bare legs and feet. 'I need a coat or something. Proper clothes.'

'Wardrobe.'

I bound over to the wardrobe. Yanking it open, I look up at a wall of elaborate work dresses, sequined gowns and fancy blouses that button down the back.

'Jesus ... do you not own a tracksuit or something?'

'Here!' She throws me her long sheepskin jacket as she dons a heavy fur coat. She grabs her phone and runs to the window.

'How do you open this safety latch?'

I pull the fitting off the latch and we push the glass pane open. Ashleigh jumps out lightly. I scramble up after her. Without my contact lenses in, I can just about make out the large hedge I have to jump over. Like a cat calculating its lithe spring, I lock my gaze on the asphalt on the far side of the bush, then jump out, gracelessly miss my step and tumble unceremoniously onto my hands and knees.

'*Ow.*'

'Over here.'

Struggling to my feet, hands and knees trickling with blood, I run to Ashleigh. We find ourselves in the internal courtyard of our building, a small children's playground enclosed by four walls of other flats and windows. We silently run a lap around the square, peering into windows for any sign of life, anyone who could help.

'Everyone is asleep, there is nowhere to go.'

'Car park?' Ashleigh asks softly.

'We'll have no phone coverage for the taxi. Plus, what if he's down there?'

Running back to Ashleigh's window, I push the open window back to an almost closed position. If the intruder comes by, he will not see that it is open, but we could still get back in if he came for us through the car park. Climbing back in would be another story, but at least we have some form of an exit.

'The taxi's on its way,' Ashleigh whispers.

'Thank God.'

'I'll try Niamh again.' The line rings out a second time.

I start trembling. 'What if he got into her room?' My voice is breaking. 'We need to go back and get her out. We need to warn her.'

'Hang on, I'll text her first. She might be afraid to make any noise if he's still in the flat. She's going to be OK. There's no way she didn't hear you made it safely to my room. She'll have locked her door.'

I stare out into the courtyard as Ashleigh texts Niamh. The blue glint from her screen seems to be beaming like a lighthouse in a storm. Surely the intruder will see it and come for us? Surely he will want to dispose of any witnesses and we are sitting ducks here, waiting for the *coup de grâce*? Where the hell is he now anyways? We crouch down motionless behind a shrub, pricking our ears for the slightest sound that could be him. My breath is trapped in my throat as we wait, too afraid to even inhale. The silence is claustrophobic.

Then I hear it. Running footsteps. I feel the hair on my forearms stand up. Slowly, we turn towards the sound, readying ourselves for the final fight.

It's Niamh. She runs up to us and drops down beside us. She is decked out in sports gear and runners. I look down at my sheepskin coat. At least one of us is dressed for the occasion.

'What happened?'

We find some words to explain the inexplicable.

'Where is that fucking taxi?' I whisper hysterically.

'He seems to be stuck,' Ashleigh says, looking at her phone. 'It's all one-way streets around here.'

We wait in silence again. Three separate times, I hear an echo that I could swear is him. At this stage he could find us just from the sound of my heart thumping through my chest. This is what it must be like to wait for your death.

We peer over the bush again.

'I can't see anything, I don't have my contacts,' I whisper.

'Me neither.'

'Yeah, me neither.'

Great. Make that three short-sighted sitting ducks. Shooting in a fish tank would be harder work than disposing of us.

Ashleigh holds up her phone screen to me. Her phone is on silent but displayed on the screen is a number calling.

'It's the taxi driver.'

'We can't answer it,' I hiss. 'If the intruder is still out here, he'll hear us.'

'The map says he's stuck on the road parallel to this one.'

My stomach drops. That's the road my bedroom gives on to.

'It's ringing again. We need to tell him to come here.'

'Give it to me.' She hands me the phone. As quietly as I can, I pick up and try to whisper directions to the driver to come around to the back road.

'I can't hear you,' replies the voice.

I murmur a decibel louder. No joy.

'Can we text him the directions?'

Ashleigh tries tapping them in. 'It's not working. He's ringing me again.'

'We're going to have to make a run for it. Do you have the number to open the car-park gate?'

'Yeah, I can activate it from my phone. Are you guys ready to run when it opens?'

We nod and swallow. That gate does not move fast, and it makes one hell of a racket when it does. Anyone in a two-street radius will hear it loud and clear. Probably even further in the dead of night.

'Here goes nothing.'

She hits the button. The old cast-iron gate begins its impossibly slow procession, its hinges screeching in protest as it inches open, one painful centimetre at a time.

'It's making too much noise.' My voice is a panicked whisper. 'He's going to hear and come for us.'

We look on helplessly, waiting for the gap to be wide enough to let us through.

'I think we can go now!' urges Ashleigh.

We spring to our feet and hurtle forward blindly, past the gate and around the corner. In the blur as we run, I notice a white van pulled up with its warning lights flashing. *Could that be him?*

'Keep going!' shouts Ashleigh.

Niamh grabs me by the arm and we dart around the second corner, arriving onto the main street.

'Is that the Hailo over there?!'

As we race up to the taxi, in our big fur coats and bare feet, the driver eyes us up and down through the car window with visible distress before hastily lockong the doors.

We hammer down on the car bonnet. 'Let us in! LET US IN!'

'Ashleigh?' he asks, peering with narrowed eyes through the thinnest gap he can crack open in the window.

'YES!' we holler.

He unlocks the doors and we bundle in.

'So where are we goi-'

'JUST DRIVE!!'

'You alright, ladies?' a male voice calls from outside the taxi.

We look up and two men dressed in uniforms are approaching, examining us suspiciously.

'Are you a garda?' Ashleigh asks loudly.

'I'm ... Wha-? Yes, I'm a garda. What are yo-?'

'Show me your badge,' replies Ashleigh without missing a beat.

'My badg-? What?' The startled garda seems disarmed by this request but proceeds to comply.

Ashleigh turns to me. 'I'm trusting no one after what happened tonight,' she mutters before taking his badge and inspecting it. 'OK, he's a garda.'

'That's what I sai-'

'We called the gardaí about twenty minutes ago. Someone broke into my flatmate's room and assaulted her.'

He looks at us in slight bewilderment for a second and sighs loudly, unaware of what happened. 'Alright then, lead the way to your flat.'

We climb out of the taxi.

'So we're not going anywhere?' asks the taxi driver, crestfallen.

This had to be so much excitement for his Tuesday night. The gardaí take his details and explain that he might be called on to give a statement.

I inhale deeply. The wail of the alarm bells running havoc in my mind are finally powering down.

We are safe.

SURVIVAL GUIDE: THE ASSAULT

It's difficult to do a checklist for what to do in the event of a rape or sexual assault. Every situation is completely unique, and it enrages me that it should be left up to women and victims to keep ourselves safe. There is only ever one party at fault in a sexual assault, and it is never the person assaulted. We should be teaching people to respect women, not telling our daughters to keep themselves out of trouble.

But until that change comes about, I'm a big believer in empowering people now. While things happen very fast and you often won't have time to think clearly, there are a few things that are good to know and that, for me, kicked in like muscle memory during the assault. These small nuggets of knowledge honestly helped save my life, and they might just help save another someday.

Know their weak spots: eyes, nose, throat, stomach, groin.

Know your hard spots: forehead, knees, elbows, knuckles, teeth, nails, sides of your hands. You hit their weak spots with your hard spots.

Fight back, if you can: this isn't always possible, particularly if your attacker is armed, so this will be a judgement call depending on the situation. But you can make it difficult for your attacker by constantly moving in different directions and thrashing about with your arms, hips and legs. Sometimes resistance can give you the element of surprise, which you can use to your advantage to get away.

Keep your vital organs protected: this is even more important if your attacker is armed. Shield your throat and face with your arms and elbows. Keep your hands in front of you and keep them moving. Keep your chin tucked down to protect your airway.

Run: as soon as you have an opening, make a run for it. Fighting will only get you so far, but the sole purpose of fighting is to free yourself from your attacker and buy yourself a couple of precious seconds to escape.

Get help: run until you find a crowded place or someone who can help you. If you can, avoid getting into a stranger's car or going into their house if they are alone, even if they offer to help.

Understand the responses to trauma: trauma triggers four different modes, depending on the situation: fight, flight, freeze or fawn. Whichever response your body adopts, understand that all four responses are equally designed to save your life:
- **Fight:** fighting or becoming aggressive towards the source of threat.
- **Flight:** running or fleeing from the situation.
- **Freeze:** becoming incapable of moving or making a decision, which usually avoids worsening the situation or minimises injuries.
- **Fawn:** trying to appease or please your abuser in order to defuse the conflict or pre-empt any violence.

Everything I've listed above is just useful knowledge to have, but remember that once the adrenaline kicks in, things happen extremely fast and your rational mind will have very little control over the situation.

Do not ever let yourself or someone else tell you that just because you froze or even complied with your abuser, that it was somehow your fault. Staying immobile is a protection, fawning is highly adaptive in survival. Your body was guided by your reptilian brain in a matter of milliseconds. It reacted in exactly the right way, given all circumstances you were facing, to save your life and minimise the damage done to you.

Start building your narrative: shame and self-blame can set in very early after an assault. Building on the above, the words you choose to describe what happened to you are so important in your future recovery, both in your internal monologue and when speaking to others. You are a survivor, not a victim.

2.

Crime Scene:

The Criminal Investigation

**Diary entry, 18 July 2019:
'We could have tripped this investigation
up at so many points.'**

We walk back towards the apartment in silent resolve. As we approach the entrance door to the building, I notice that something is sticking out of my bedroom window. I squint to make out what it is. Stepping closer, I realise it's the window-pane. It has been taken fully off the safety latch and is standing wide open at a 90-degree angle. Here comes the first wave of nausea.

'That's my window.'

'That's your apartment?'

'Yes, that's how he must have gotten in.' He? That won't do. It. *Beast*.

On the other side of the window is a pitch-black void.

The second garda peers inside. 'It's empty.'

The first garda turns to us and explains they had been called for another burglary down the road. The team responding to our call will be here soon. While he places a call to the station to confirm this, my two flatmates huddle next to each other as if they are cold. Niamh's eyes are enormous.

'Are you OK, Sarah? Did he do anything to you?'

I struggle to remember the order of events. I begin to describe it to them, delivering the story flatly, like I'm recounting some distant recollection of a movie. *That's insane, that didn't actually happen to me, right?* When I get to the sexual assault, they both weep silently. Niamh whispers my name repeatedly under her breath, tears streaming down her face. *Why are they crying?* I feel nothing. As if a trip switch has been flicked, shutting down my emotions. *Why am I not crying? Should I be?*

I later read about this reaction in Dr Bessel van de Kolk's book *The Body Keeps the Score*[2] – a brilliant book that I cannot recommend highly enough to understand the science behind trauma. He describes how traumatised people often find it difficult to speak about how they are internally experiencing the effects of trauma. Instead, they will focus on telling the external story: what was done to them, not how they feel about it. It is simply too much for the human mind to process, particularly in the immediate aftermath of what they have just survived.

The garda finishes his call and looks at us with concern. 'Let's get you girls out of the cold.'

Is it cold? I can't feel anything.

We point out that we don't have keys, so the second garda goes back with Ashleigh to the square where we hid earlier to get in through her window. As we wait, the first garda asks questions about what happened. I describe the events again. His head jolts up.

---

2 *The Body Keeps the Score: Brain, Mind, and Body in the Healing of Trauma*, Bessel van der Kolk , M.D. (Penguin Random House, 2015).

'You were sexually assaulted?'

I nod.

The effects of shock are now in full swing. I sense I should be in pain, but instead a warm blanket of numbness has draped itself around my body. An overwhelming sense of calm has taken over. I'm in a dream-like state, which I would later understand to be dissociation. It's quite pleasant, in fact. I'm afraid to disturb it. The smallest motion, even speaking, feels like an Olympian task. Everything is warm and extremely comfortable. I would have happily sat down on the pavement and never gotten up again. I have no idea what psychological effects are coming after this, but somehow I don't think they're going to be pleasant, so long may this last.

Ashleigh buzzes open the door and the garda gently ushers us inside. Walking through the front hall, the atmosphere in our apartment is completely different from before the attack. It doesn't feel like the same place. I reluctantly push open the door of my bedroom, half expecting to see my dead body behind it. I flick on the light. A black baseball cap is lying on the floor where the struggle took place, defiantly staring up at me. So I didn't dream it.

'That's not mine.'

'The baseball cap?'

'Yep.'

'Alright, don't touch it. Is anything else here not yours?'

I scan the room and my eyes land on the remains of the potted plant that used to sit on my windowsill, now trampled on the floor along with scattered earth and the broken shards of its clay pot. I start piecing together what must have happened before I woke up. Beast must have opened the safety latch, climbed in and knocked down my plant as he grappled with the black-out curtains. *Asshole.* I loved that plant.

'Pretty sure those footprints on the windowsill are his.'

Walking around the bed, I notice the newly empty spots around my room.

'My handbag is gone. My phone … my work iPhone, too. My iPad.' I turn around. 'And I had a little gold jewellery box here, it's also gone.' Talk about adding insult to injury. 'He took everything.'

A pang of sadness pierces through my warm blanket of calm. That Kate Spade handbag was a gift from my mother for qualifying as a solicitor. I'm not big into material things (sure we only got it on sale in the Kildare Village outlet), but the sentimental value of it was priceless. Despite it only being a week old, I already treasured it as a symbol of that achievement and of my mom marking the occasion. Not to mention that it contained my entire life, from my ID to my wallet, make-up bag, perfume, work pass and all the cards that would be such a pain to get replaced.

Sigh – one thing at a time, Sarah.

Back in the living room, the gardaí are growing in numbers. One of them smells of cigarettes. My brain is not happy about this, shrieking internally at the smell. My heart rate takes off like a rocket.

So that's a PTSD[3] trigger, interesting.

I breathe through my mouth and try to put as much distance as humanly possible between him and me. I can actually tell by smell alone the different areas where he has stood in our living room. The internal shrieking intensifies.

Ashleigh and Niamh are speaking on their phones to their families. *My family.* No point in calling them. There's nothing they can do right now, let

---

3 Post-traumatic stress disorder (PTSD). I'll cover this in detail in Chapter 4.

them have their sleep. The last thing I need is for them all to pile into a car at 4.00am and get into an accident as they hurtle down the motorway. They won't have to come and clear out my room after all, at least that thought gives me some comfort. My stream of consciousness is interrupted by a beautiful Irish moment, as Niamh comes up to me holding the kettle and softly asks, 'You'll have a cuppa tea, Sarah, will ya?'

'Thanks, Niamh, I don't think I could keep it down.'

Instinctively, I feel like I shouldn't be drinking anything. I don't want anything touching anywhere that Beast touched – which is pretty much everywhere. Drinking, even comforting tea, would disturb this delectable blanket of shock that I am so gratefully cloaked in. One of the gardaí comes over to us and explains that we'll have to go to the station to give a proper statement, but for now they'll take our details and let us get some rest. Distant recollections of my criminal law studies begin floating to the surface, including random pieces on criminal evidence and procedure.

I'm extremely conscious that Beast is still out there and that every hour, every detail, counts. During sleep, the brain processes memories and filters out certain information. Sleep deprivation and interrupted sleep patterns impact this even more – memory consolidation is impaired as the brain essentially does not have time to create new pathways for the information learnt. When you add trauma to the mix (which, for information, is what is happening in the dissociative state), the emotional brain can sometimes fragment or even rewrite parts of the narrative if it gets overwhelmed by the traumatic experience. It is so important to know this, not just in a rape or sexual violence scenario but in any case that involves trauma. That's why it's essential to get your story recorded in detail as soon as possible, to capture all the minutiae before the brain starts blurring the memory further.

'I think we should give our full statements now,' I say obstinately.

'OK, if you're sure, but maybe you should get some sleep first?'

Ah, sleep. I don't think I'll ever know what that is again. The idea of letting go of consciousness right now is unfathomable.

'No, it has to be tonight.'

'OK, I'll just take your details now. What's your full name?'

'Sarah Grace.'

'Age?'

'Twenty-eight.'

'Occupation?'

'Solicitor. The three of us are.'

After a few more practical questions, he goes to check on his colleagues. I hear him admonish one, telling him to be careful around the evidence. I follow them into my room to get some proper clothes before we go to the station.

'I'm sorry, Miss, you can't go in there. This is the crime scene.'

'But I just went in a few minutes ago.'

'I know, but we need to preserve all the evidence of the crime scene. We can't touch anything before Forensics get here.'

'Look, I just want to get some clothes if we're going to the station. You're wearing sterile gloves now, so I can point at the drawer and you open it. I'll pull out the top item and touch nothing else.'

He indulges me. I pull out a simple long black dress, one of my favourite pieces for a casual summer evening. It's soft and loose, long enough to cover my battered knees and with a wrap-over top I can drape gently around my sore skin.

Once dressed, I can't find the garda who took my details, so I turn to one of his junior colleagues and ask if I should go to hospital. He slowly blinks as I explain the assault to him, and then shouts across to the other side of the room.

'Uh, chief? CHIEF? Did you know she was sexually assaulted?'

Well, if my neighbours didn't know what happened before, they know now. The whole block surely does after that announcement. The Big Chief gives him the deepest eye-roll I've ever witnessed. Before he can stride over to us, another garda gently leans over, his voice full of kindness and sympathy.

'I wouldn't really recommend it, to be honest. It can be quite invasive, you know.'

I nod, both relieved and deflated. The kindness in his tone registers, but something doesn't feel right. In hindsight, it is astounding that none of us had the faintest idea about what to do in such a critical situation. While he absolutely meant well, and his intentions were excellent, if I hadn't got the medical examination that night, it would have tanked the trial.

I ask my flatmates for a second opinion.

'That's definitely not right, Sarah. You need to go to hospital.' I hear them mention digital rape, but it barely registers.

I go back to the Big Chief with this.

'OK, we'll arrange it all for you. We'll go to the station first because we need to ring the doctor who's on call and it might take them a while to arrive.'

The girls are gathering their things from their rooms. I ask the Big Chief how long, approximately, the statements and hospital appointment will take.

'At least a couple of hours.'

The girls glance up from packing their bags.

'OK, it's just that we need to be at work in four hours.'

The gardaí in our living room all stop what they're doing and look up at us in unison, equal parts incredulous and disapproving.

'Ashleigh, can you email my team to let them know I won't be in until this afternoon?' I pause. 'Actually, do you know what? I was sexually assaulted and nearly murdered. Surely I can take the day off?'

The gardaí's jaws hit the floor.

'Lawyers,' I hear one of them mutter under his breath.

Fair comment, really.

* * *

On our way to the station, the garda driving us seems tense. His posture is impeccable. My God, I've never seen someone sit up that straight. He drives so slowly that we get overtaken by a cyclist, carefully taking each speed ramp like the three of us are made of glass.

At the station, we're ushered through the lobby, where a homeless man is sleeping, and straight into a windowless room. There's nothing here except a battered fake-leather armchair. The girls gently nudge me towards it to sit down.

'NOT THAT CHAIR!' bellow the guards.

We stare in bemusement at them.

'We'll bring in some chairs,' they mutter sheepishly and leave.

We lean over the armrest to examine it more closely.

'Do those look like nail scratches to you?'

I shrug. 'I don't even want to know.'

I'm called up first to give my statement. The Big Chief is taking it, and he introduces me to his colleague, I'll call her Jessica. As the crime involves a sexual offence, I'm entitled to have a female garda present when giving my evidence. I actually feel very safe speaking to the Big Chief alone, but at this stage any form of protest feels like way too much effort, so I smile meekly at her. Giving my statement is a slow process. You've read my story, it's a long one to tell. All I can think about is ensuring Beast gets caught. I leave nothing out, knowing that every little detail could help. The potential trial is also in the back of my mind, much further down the line, so I'm determined to be as accurate as possible.

The Big Chief is writing everything down by hand, so I have to pause frequently. I ask if it would be faster to type it, but apparently only two Garda stations in the country are fitted with that 'equipment' (*laptops?*). He explains that he'll have to type up my statement after we're done. Baffling.

My memory is already beginning to fail me. They ask me if I heard Beast speak.

I pause. 'I'm not sure. He shushed me. I think he may have said something, but I don't remember what.'

Big Chief asks for a physical description. Again, I have to rack my brain.

'I don't know. I think he was white, definitely not black or Asian. Possibly Latin American? Italian? I think he was tanned. I only properly saw his face for a second. He had stubble. I wouldn't be able to recognise him.'

The difficulty I found, with an event as horrific as this, was how to put words on the unspeakable. My brain was trying to make sense of the senseless, to put some meaning on the unfathomable. Each word I spoke out loud seemed to crystallise the memory into place. I would later understand that the words I chose that night would help seal the narrative in my mind forever, hence why it was so important to acknowledge what I had endured head-on.

'It was very violent.' I mentally scour my vocabulary, trying to find the words to best describe the unsavoury motion. 'He – rammed – his fingers inside me. Extremely violently. With the force of a punch, I guess.'

I finish my statement and return to the scratched-armchair room as the Big Chief goes to check on the status of the doctor on-call. Ashleigh and Niamh are there, they've already given their own statements. As we wait, I can see that Jessica is scrambling for something to say. She eventually settles on, 'I'm so sorry.'

I just smile weakly again.

The Big Chief comes back, lugging an enormous bin bag full of T-shirts and tracksuits behind him. He hands it to me, telling me to find my size. They'll have to keep my clothes after the medical examination, so I'm to take these with me to the hospital. He explains that another colleague of his will drive me to the sexual assault clinic while my flatmates wait for me in the station. Ashleigh and Niamh protest strongly at this – 'Obviously we're going with her' – but the Big Chief apologises and explains it is standard procedure and I can't bring them with me.

I nod. 'It's fine, you guys stay here.'

'Should we call your parents while you're at the hospital?'

'No. There's no point, there's nothing they can do right now. I'll call them once the hospital and police pieces are done. Right now, let's focus on getting those out of the way.'

'I really think we should call them, Sarah. They would want to know.'

'No.'

They sigh. 'OK.'

The garda due to drive me to hospital finally arrives. Well, *bonjour.* He's the size of a wardrobe, just one of his shoulders must be double the width of my head. There's an aura about him that immediately makes me feel safe in his presence. He's like a giant guard bear, a human shield with pecs the size of Leinster. Bear nods in our direction and grumbles something that I think is a cross between a *Hello* and a grunt. If anyone else tries to attack me and I can't fend them off myself, he'll definitely be able to. I'm half-hoping we do run into Beast now. *He'd be minced meat,* I think gleefully. The Big Chief explains that Bear will be driving me and Jessica to the Sexual Assault Treatment Unit (SATU) at the Rotunda hospital. Bear seems to speak only in grunts. Somehow, I find that comforting. He growls something in gruff-ish and signals us to walk with him. I run after his heels obediently, like my life depends on it.

SURVIVAL GUIDE: THE CRIMINAL INVESTIGATION

You have just been through an incredibly traumatic event, and you may not want to call the police for a number of reasons. But I would recommend that you do so, as at this stage it is just about getting the evidence before it is destroyed, and any decision to prosecute will not be made until later. However, each case is unique. Ultimately, this is *your* decision. All I can tell you is that I am glad I reported the assault immediately, as it meant my attacker was found and arrested, and that my statement and the evidence were strong, which proved crucial in the trial.

It's hard to have to think about a trial so soon after the assault, but unfortunately now is when the strategy and gathering of evidence for court begins. If you do call the gardaí, there are a few things you should know to watch out for. This applies to any police investigation, but particularly to cases of rape or sexual violence, where evidence is so crucial.

If possible, stay where you are: leave everything exactly where it was until the police arrive. Avoid moving things as the place where the assault happened will be cordoned off as the crime scene. It is extremely important that this is not tampered with in any way, otherwise the evidence gathered from it could be rejected at trial.

Do not touch anything in the crime scene without sterile equipment: no one should be walking through the area or touching anything in it unless they are wearing the appropriate gear (i.e. sterile gloves, shoe covers) so as not to disturb any footprints, fingerprints, DNA or other evidence. If an item must be touched, tweezers or tongs should be used and it should be placed straight into a plastic forensics bag. This rule applies to the gardaí as much as to anyone else present. Whether you are the victim or a witness, do not be shy about telling any person, police or civilian, to put on PPE before they approach the crime scene.

Keep the clothes you are wearing on you until the forensic examination in hospital: if you need to put more clothes on, avoid anything skin-tight to preserve any DNA or evidence that may be on your skin. Be comfortable and, if possible, choose clothes you don't love. (The gardaí will take them as evidence and although they will be returned to you, it could be years later.) Even if you really want to, try not to wash or touch any evidence on your body until the sexual assault clinic staff have gathered all the medical evidence from your person. (See more on this in the Survival Guide at the end of Chapter 3.)

You can bring a support person with you when giving your statement at the Garda station: it is very important that this person is not a witness to the crime. This is to avoid the perpetrator's Defence team later arguing in court that you copied each other's stories. If you are worried about bringing a family member, the Dublin Rape Crisis Centre offers a wonderful accompaniment service to inform and support you if you want to make a statement in relation to sexual violence (and later on in court – see Chapter 8). You can contact them directly or ask the gardaí to call them for you.

You can request that a female garda be present when giving your statement: this is purely to make sure you are as comfortable as possible and has absolutely no bearing or impact on the statement itself. You decide what feels right for you.

Try to give your statement as soon as possible after the crime: once you sleep, your memories may become further blurred or less accurate. You may be told that you can wait until the next day, but you should insist on having it taken immediately, if you feel able to do so. This will not only make your statement more contemporaneous for the purposes of the trial (and therefore harder for the Defence counsel to argue that you didn't remember something correctly), it will also help start your healing process by putting your own words on what you have endured. Tell your story, leave nothing out. No detail is too small.

If you have any injuries, ensure the gardaí take photos of them: this includes bruising, cuts, grazes, or redness on your skin if you were pinned down. They won't take photos of any intimate parts of your body. Do not worry if you don't have any physical markings, as you don't need them to prove lack of consent, but if you were hurt this should absolutely be recorded. As above, no detail is too small in the investigation.

If there were any witnesses, they should all give statements too: if you were at a party with friends, for example, and they saw you leave or witnessed something that could help prove what you are saying, they should give their statement immediately as well. The only evidence that won't be admissible in court is anything deemed 'hearsay', which is any-thing they were *told* happened but did not actually *witness* (for example, if they weren't at the party but you later told them, 'I was raped'). What they *can* testify to in that example is what state you were in, or any injuries they noticed on your face or body when they saw you, because they actually witnessed that first-hand.

Remember that your statement will be used in a trial, if there is one: you will tell the gardaí in your own words what happened, and they will write it down word for word. Your statement will be a key part of the Book of Evidence (which is a folder containing all of the evidence that the Prosecution intends to rely on in court), so it is crucial that it is as accurate as possible and that you can stand over every single thing you say. You will be given a copy of your statement ahead of the trial to re-read and refresh your memory.

Give as much detail as possible: times, addresses, locations, names, or anything you noticed about the place or the attacker that could be useful. As painful as some details may be, remember they will be so important for the jury, who were not present at the crime scene, to have as clear a picture as possible of what happened.

Be very clear on what you are sure about and what you are not sure about: if you are not certain of something, say so and explain why. For example, you can say, 'I think it was around 2.00am, but I am not exactly sure', or 'I know he had tattoos because I saw them on his arms'. This will help with credibility and show that you are not guessing at things. At trial, you will have to be able to stand over every single word said in your statement, so being honest and accurate now is crucial.

Take your time giving your statement: it is completely OK to pause as you give your statement for as long as you need, and to think before you speak. Statements can take hours. Make sure to get the words right. If you say something and then realise that it wasn't quite right, do not be afraid to correct it. The gardaí will cross it out and write it again, then you will both initial every correction to show you agreed with it (and that it was not changed after you left, for example).

Think your words through carefully: when you are giving your statement, if something could be open to interpretation, always clarify. Use the plainest words possible, because Defence teams may try to twist their meaning. For example, in my case, they analysed to death the term I used in my statement to describe the violence of the assault: *the force of a punch.* They used it to argue that a punch is 'not sexual' in nature, therefore my attacker's intentions were not sexual either. Another common example is attributing thoughts or motivation to the attacker (for example, 'he seemed surprised' or 'he didn't mean it'). The Defence could try to use this to argue in court that the perpetrator did not have the requisite intention to commit this crime. Avoid speaking about the perpetrator's state of mind.

Be extremely clear on consent: it is critical that your statement notes that you did not consent to what was done to you, even if it is painfully obvious from the facts. This will ensure that if you decide you do want to pursue this further, the option of a trial is open to you.

Make sure the gardaí read your statement back to you and ask you to sign it (and also to initial any corrections, as above): again, this is a legal requirement for the statement to be valid and used in the Book of Evidence for court.

Ask for a contact person in the gardaí: they will normally give you a contact person and a phone number. You'll want someone you can contact if you have any follow-up questions. You will usually be allocated a Family Liaison Officer (FLO), who will be your main point of contact regarding the investigation and potential trial.

Give a follow-up statement, if necessary: certain memories will inevitably come to you only days later. This is normal, that's how trauma works. When this happens, write it all down immediately. Then go back to the Garda station with your notes and give a second statement. This will be added to your first statement and they will usually start it with, *Since my previous statement, I remember the following.* Do not feel that you cannot go back in several times to give more statements because it will somehow undermine your first statement. It won't. This is criminal evidence, so leave no stone unturned.

If you come across more evidence after the investigation, call your contact in the police or FLO: try to avoid touching it with your hands, instead use a Ziploc or plastic bag to bag it until the gardaí collect it, so any forensic evidence does not get damaged.

Remember, you can always give a statement much later: if you did not give a statement at the time of the assault, there is nothing preventing you from giving one at a later point in time. I would encourage you to speak with either the Dublin Rape Crisis Centre or Legal Aid Board (which is free for certain sexual violence victims – more on this in the Survival Guide for Chapter 7) and write up a 'mock' statement first. This will help clarify your memory of events and ensure you have all the facts.

You should ask to be taken to a sexual assault treatment unit (SATU) immediately: it is crucial that you get evidence of the assault as soon as possible after it happens. You are most certainly exhausted, but this is the most important thing you can do for your own sake. The SATU will provide a pregnancy test, anti-HIV medication and tend to any other injuries you have, for free. They are trained professionals who will treat you with the utmost care and make you feel safe and respected. (For full details on this, see Chapter 3.)

3.

Stop, Drop and Roll:
The Medical Evidence

Diary entry, 18 July 2019:
'Thank God I went there. It was like reclaiming my dignity and power, one limb at a time.'

On arrival at the Rotunda hospital, Bear buzzes the bell. We wait for a few minutes outside the big, black metal door; it feels like a drugs bust. I'm calm but slightly on edge now, like something is about to happen. We're buzzed in and I'm surprised to see quite a large number of people waiting inside. The Sexual Assault Treatment Unit (SATU) is a couple of doors down. Bear power marches over to reception, shouldering his way through them all, barks a few words at the receptionist and I'm quickly ushered into a separate room. No messing with this guy.

I'm told the doctor and someone from the Dublin Rape Crisis Centre will come shortly. Then everything is eerily quiet. I sit on the edge of the cheap leather sofa, looking out the window. Dawn is breaking. This time yesterday, I was watching the same sun rise from the car window as we drove to Galway. What a strange thought that seems now. This is the first time I've been alone since the attack happened. I can't take it in. My brain just won't process it. I'm in the waiting room of the *Sexual Assault* clinic. Someone from the *Rape Crisis Centre* is coming. This cannot be happening to me. *To me.* I'm always so careful. I never walk down dark alleys. I always hold my drink with my hand over the glass to make sure no one spikes it. I own a pepper spray, for crying out loud.

A sense of shame is beginning to bubble up. What if people from work find out? What will they think? I can't be branded with this.

* * *

The accompanier from the Dublin Rape Crisis Centre arrives ten minutes later, introduces herself and offers to wait with me, if I would like her to.

'You don't have to speak. We don't have to say anything. You can just close your eyes and rest.'

Thank sweet merciful dancing Moses for that. We sit in silence.

It's not long after that when a very jovial nurse pops her head in through the door and smiles at me. I get up and follow her into the examination room, where two other women are waiting, a doctor and her supervisor. They're all smiles and warmth as they immediately put me at ease and invite me to sit. The supervising doctor explains that the junior doctor is training to do these examinations on her own. She then walks me very clearly, step-by-step, through the process ahead. They'll start with a number of questions about what happened and any relevant medical information, then they will perform the examination itself, which they'll do one limb at a time so as not to overwhelm me. They'll take note of every cut, bruise and other mark on a body map they have on their medical chart. They explain why each step is important for the police investigation and for the evidence, should there be a trial. Full marks for this welcome party, there isn't one shred of pity, just empathy and humanity coming through in buckets.

If I was calm at the apartment, the sensation I'm feeling now is bordering on inertia. They could aim a missile at my head and I wouldn't bat an eyelid. I'm vaguely trying to remember if I was possibly sedated at the Garda station. (Obviously, I wasn't.) As the supervising doctor runs through the questions with me, all quite straightforward, the junior doctor takes notes. I notice that her hand is shaking. *Holy crap, she's even more scared than I am.* This makes me sit up. I can do something to help. *I can be useful!*

I smile gently at her between questions. 'You're doing great.' Wow, my voice is husky.

She looks up in bewilderment, and there's a moment of connection. We share a look of relief and gratitude, as the nurse and supervising doctor beam in the background.

We move on to the medical examination and I'm asked to slip on a hospital gown. They reassure me that it will make the process a lot easier for me, too. We start with the feet and work our way up. When we reach my knees the three of them gather around at exactly the right distance, not too close, not too far away, and gasp at the state of my legs in united coos that would put all Irish mammies to shame.

'Oh my darling, your poor knees!'

'Oh, no. He didn't do that. That was self-inflicted.'

Three confused pairs of eyes peek up at me from the medical chart.

'I did that to myself when I jumped out the window. I missed my landing. For a yoga teacher, I don't have the best balance.'

They laugh uncertainly. I make a mental note to stop cracking jokes as a defence mechanism.

The medical examination is thorough. The doctors and nurse gather every single piece of Beast's DNA from each millimetre of my body. I didn't realise how much there was, from his blood on my lips and underneath my fingernails, to skin cells gathered from combing through my hair. The whole process is incredibly dignified and professional. They gently ask me to lift the gown over one limb at a time, leaving the rest of my body covered: first between my wrist and my elbow, then my elbow to shoulder, shoulder to collarbone, and so on. They take swabs inside my mouth. They write down every cut, every bruise, including the hand-shaped ones on my throat. I really didn't dream it. They clean my wounds as they go. Every time they find a new injury, they get excited and clamour 'We got him! We got him!', because they know this will add to the DNA evidence and to the credibility of my story come the trial.

I'm so glad I didn't listen to the well-meaning garda. Thank God I came here tonight. Thank God I didn't drink that tea or take a shower. In hindsight, it's unbelievable that no one told me not to do those things. If I had, we would have lost key evidence that could have cost us the trial.

From the distance I have now, I can clearly see the invaluable importance of the SATU process. It's not just about collecting evidence, it was about my healing too. I know for a fact that my recovery would have taken a very different course had I not gone there that night, and I'll never be able to thank the SATU squad enough for what they did.

When they move on to the internal examination, they note that the cut from his fingernail is several inches long. Before I can even begin to freak out, the nurse registers my eyes getting wider and launches into an enthusiastic tribute to the female body.

'There is so much blood flow down there. That will heal in less than a day. It'll be like it never even happened. Your body is just incredible, you know? It can heal itself from the worst of traumas.'

Her words bring me a lot of strength and comfort.

'I wish my mind was that powerful,' I answer quietly.

'Oh, it is, honey. This will not be you for the rest of your life. You'll have small moments of blissful forgetting, and they will get longer and longer. One day this will all be behind you.'

As I slide the gown down past my collarbone, the doctor calls out a bite mark on my chest. I look down and it's all I can do not to faint. Very distinct teeth marks are glowering up at me, purple against my skin. My breathing accelerates.

'I don't remember him biting me.'

'Don't you worry, my dear. That will heal in no time, and he didn't break the skin, it's not bleeding. You put up an amazing fight.'

'What if there's something else that he did that I don't remember?' My lip is quivering now.

'It's extremely unlikely. You did feel him on your neck, but with the adrenaline your pain threshold was probably a lot higher. You're very lucid now, and you gave him one hell of a thrashing. You got yourself out and you should feel very proud.'

She explains that they will also have me take a pregnancy test, even though there's obviously no need for one in this situation. But it's standard procedure. I'm offered a hepatitis B shot and every STI medication under the sun, to make sure nothing comes of his bloodied hand having come into contact with the cut. They also give me a note for my employer to say I'll be off work for a month.

'Oh, I don't need a month, maybe just today and tomorrow. I can go back in on Monday, latest.'

Stunned silence again. I'm starting to think this whole approach to work hours is not deemed acceptable by normal people. I'll have to look into that.

'You really need the month, honey. It probably hasn't hit you yet how much you've been through.'

'I just have a lot of work on at the moment. Next week is going to be very busy,' I add hastily.

She bites her lip. 'OK, we'll put a week down, but call us any time and we can extend it.'

The medical examination ends and they hand me a toothbrush and a towel. *Finally.* While they complete my file, I'm shown to the showers. As I take off my clothes, there's blood on the dress and my underwear. *Wonderful.*

I let the water hit between my shoulder blades. It's searing hot and my bruised skin groans in protest, but I welcome it. It feels like lava, burning my skin away. *Burn every trace of him away.* I don't know how long I stood there, staring into nothingness, in this blank dissociated state, letting the scalding water cleanse my body. Maybe if I stayed in here long enough, it would cleanse my soul, too.

Eventually, I step out and risk a glance into the mirror. I do not recognise the person staring back at me. The tops of her shoulders are crimson from where the steaming water has landed. It is hard to make eye contact with her. I avoid her gaze, and instead let her inspect my neck, the sides of my face and my collarbone. The hand marks on my throat are still visible, glaring angrily through the red skin. She too can't bring herself to look further down than my neckline, for fear of catching sight of the vicious bite mark again.

I pick up the clothes given to me by the Big Chief and pull them on before looking into the mirror again. If I didn't recognise the girl in the towel before, she is totally unrecognisable now. Donning a tracksuit, white T-shirt and hoodie, pale and gaunt-faced, hair pulled back into a ponytail, she looks like she stepped out of a methadone clinic. I can't see *me* anywhere.

Where are you?

I don't know if the old Sarah is ever coming back, or if she's been replaced by this sad ghost forever. I feel like I should cry, but I got nothing.

With a deep sigh, I put my own clothes – my last connection to the old Sarah – into the plastic evidence bag and seal it. It feels like the most anti-climactic funeral ever.

I step out down the corridor and into another room. A daunting scene awaits on the other side of the door. The doctors and nurse are seated at a table, all facing me. There is an empty chair opposite them. The two gardaí, Bear and Jessica, are standing behind the chair, also turned to face me. I stand there awkwardly, feeling extremely vulnerable. It's like facing the papal conclave for an inquisition. The supervising doctor invites me to sit down, so I walk to the centre of the room to sit into the empty chair, flanked by Bear and Jessica. The doctor explains that we have to run through my statement for the file.

'Again? I already gave one to the guards. Can't you use that?'

'No, unfortunately. We don't share files with the Garda. This will be your personal file, there will be no typed copy and it will remain with SATU until the trial. We have to take it for the trial.'

'Right.'

'Can you tell us what happened?'

'OK.' Oh *boy*, here we go again.

I start recounting my story for what feels like the eleventh time. In reality, it is more like the fourth. That said, I cannot stress enough the importance of going through this process. As draining and painful as it is, it is like sucking the poison out of a snake bite. It must be done, or else the poison will run wild in your body and mind and cause even more pain and havoc in the long term. I call it the purge (enticing, right?) because that's exactly what it feels like. Your body is sore, your jaw hurts from speaking so much, you want to curl up into a ball and die, but if you can get through this, you will know for life that your inner strength is not something to be messed with. No one will ever be able to take that power away from you again.

As I recount my tale in this dark room, the atmosphere is sombre. You could cut through the tension with a knife. I'm not sure why exactly. Maybe it's the room, maybe it's the dynamic between the doctors and the gardaí. The doctors aren't smiling anymore. I'm still in a total state of shock, but when I look down, my hands are grasping each other for dear life, knuckles white from the pressure. The story-telling process is excruciating, it feels like it will never end, each word so heavy that I want to stop talking mid-sentence.

I eventually reach the point in the story where I bit off a piece of Beast's hand. The silence is suddenly broken by a low growl behind me.

'Good woman.'

The doctors' surprised eyes fly up in unison. I look back and the voice belongs to Bear. Bear can speak! There's a split second of complete silence, a gasp hanging weightless in mid-air, and then it's broken by the tinkling sound of laughter. It's nervous laughter at first, but laughter is laughter, and it's healing. I am basking in it. Like a broken spell, the austere silence is gone, and we all breathe an audible sigh of relief.

* * *

When we get back into the car, Bear drives quietly for a while, before speaking up for the second time. It's much less of a grunt now, it turns out he can speak in sentences after all.

'You did amazing back there, you really did yourself proud. Not everybody would fight back like you did. You got yourself out, and your flatmates too. You should feel really proud.'

I nod and settle further back into the car seat, clutching the seams of my new hoodie close to my chin. Man, I'm tired.

We drive in silence, watching the hustle and bustle of a world that's starting to wake up. There's a lot of traffic. Looking through the window, I'm struck by how I could be dead right now, and Dublin would be no different. That woman on the corner there would still be battling to balance her oversized bag on the pram handle. That man with his nose buried in the newspaper would still be sipping his cup of Barry's tea on his way to work. The sky would still be blue (or grey, it is Dublin after all), and life would still go on, utterly unchanged. It's a sobering thought.

They have no idea. They're rushing to work, getting their coffees, speeding away on the pavements towards their busy schedules and filled-up inboxes. It hits me that this must happen every day. I think of the thousands of women and men and people who have walked this path before me. They too have maybe watched the world carry on, unaffected, like this life-changing traumatic event that has rocked their existence to its very core never happened.

* * *

Back at the Garda station, my flatmates are waiting for me in the lobby. The homeless man has woken up and is slowly shuffling around the room. He actually looks like E.T., wrapped head-to-toe in an enormous grey blanket and staggering from side to side. He seems to be emitting a low guttural wail, maybe he's humming to himself? He doesn't seem like much of a threat, but my eyes are glued to him, watching in mistrust for any sudden movement. I only release my gaze for a few seconds at a time when someone else walks by, then go back to surveying him. Despite the eerie calm from the shock, something is stirring in my body, a primal urge to stay alert that is so deeply rooted in the abyss of my subconsciousness, it's like an ancient reptile slowly awakening from its slumber.

The girls offer to call my parents again. I shake my head, it's still too early. The Big Chief comes out to meet us. My eyes are still riveted towards E.T., unblinking, as he explains that the forensics team is still going through the crime scene, so we can't go back to the apartment.

'It'll be a while yet.'

He mentions a hotel a few streets down which has a quiet tearoom tucked upstairs. We can wait it out there. Instinctively, I go to look it up. (That cliché that women can't read maps originated from me – I depend on Google Maps to find my way even around the corner.) I reach into my pocket for my phone and remember.

'Oh yeah, fuck.'

There was my first moment of blissful forgetting. The nurse from SATU may have been on to something.

The hotel is only two streets away, but I am so damn tired I feel like we're setting off on a quest to slay a dragon. Just as I contemplate how feasible it would be to curl up on the street and sit there forever, E.T. shuffles towards us again. I groan internally. *Never mind.*

As I walk down this very familiar street, one I walk every week, I feel like a fish out of water. No coat, no handbag, no phone, no wallet, nothing to hold on to. I feel so bare and exposed I might as well be naked, and I don't know what to do with my hands. We set off to find this hotel.

* * *

The hotel lobby is a dainty little thing, with slightly too ornate sofas made of plush emerald-green fabric and dark oak finishing. Ashleigh called her brother, and he's arrived there before us and got us sodas, sweet tea and pastries from the lobby bar. He explains that it counters the drop in your blood-sugar after shock, although I don't think I could keep anything down. I hold the teacup in both hands, the heat emanating from it mimicking the warm shock blanket still cloaking my body. I decide to wait until 8.00am before calling my parents.

We contemplate our surroundings with vacant looks, shell-shocked. Everything feels surreal. Wednesday morning is in full swing, yesterday I was in the office, the day before in Galway. We should be getting ready for work right now.

'Are you guys actually going to work?'

'Not a hope. Those guards thought we were actually insane. I think maybe we are.'

I laugh dryly.

'The looks on their faces when you told them we were lawyers.'

More giggling.

'I wonder if they were losing their minds taking down my statement. I was trying to be so precise for the investigation. I kept making them correct my statement to record the exact minute everything happened. I made them rewrite entire sentences,' Ashleigh sniggers.

'Can you imagine how much of a pain we were for them? They're probably more traumatised than you are.'

The four of us are in convulsions now.

'Was it me or was that guard that drove you to the hospital really hot?'

'God, yeah.'

As the morning goes on, we're breaking our sides laughing – at our battle against Ashleigh's blanket caught in the door, at my wardrobe panic moment, at the taxi fiasco, at the armchair and E.T. in the Garda station.

'I think I'm mentally unwell to be laughing so soon after the attack.'

Ashleigh's brother shrugs. 'That's strength, Sarah.'

'Right, it's eight o'clock. Can I borrow your phone?'

Ashleigh hands it to me. Deep breath. I've got to break this to them super-gently. I dial the number.

'Hello?'

Cue the yoga teacher voice.

'Hi Dad, it's me. You OK? Hope I'm not waking you.'

'No, we're good. Are you OK? This isn't your number.'

'Yes.' I hesitate. 'Listen, I'm just calling to let you know something happened. I am *absolutely fine*,' I say before he can even take in a sharp inhale. I repeat the words even more slowly. 'I. Am. Absolutely. Fine. But I thought you guys would want to know there was a break-in at our flat last night. My phone was stolen, which is why I'm calling you from this number. We're all OK, we are just waiting for the police to go through the flat before we can go back.'

'Jesus.'

'But it's OK, no one got hurt.'

Damn, even I'm convinced by my performance. It's a pity you can't bottle shock. I need to remember how to do this for the relaxation part of my next yoga session. Ashleigh and Niamh are gawking at me in utter bewilderment. I sheepishly turn my back to them and walk towards a corner of the lounge.

'Well, actually, he attacked me, but we all got out OK. I am absolutely fine though, don't worry. I gave him a good thrashing. He came out worse than I did.' I pause. I can't help myself. 'I bit a piece of his hand off,' I say, almost proudly.

'Jesus. Wow. Jesus ...' He sounds hypnotised. 'But you're sure you're OK?'

'Yeah, absolutely. We're just waiting for the police to wrap up before we go home, and I'll give you an update then.'

'OK, wow, yeah. Do you have somewhere to go?'

'Yes, don't worry. I'll stay with one of the girls. We're all in dire need of food and sleep.'

'OK ...' Still stunned. 'OK, I love you.'

'I love you, too.'

I hang up the call and walk back to my incredulous flatmates. *And the Oscar goes to – Sarah Grace. Thank you, thank you.*

'Sometimes being a yoga teacher has its advantages,' I say in response to their speechlessness.

They laugh again, nervously this time. We continue chatting and laughing for a few more minutes before Ashleigh hands me her phone.

'Your dad's calling you back.'

Oh boy. I pick up.

'JESUS CHRIST, SARAH! You were so calm that what you said didn't hit me until after you hung up. HOW ARE YOU SO CALM? Should we be coming over?! Are you sure you're OK? Your mother is beside herself. We're packing up now and will be there this afternoon.'

'No, don't do that. I'm fine, I promise. You guys are due back tomorrow, right? Don't be rushing back. I don't think I can cope with it, to be honest. I don't even know how much longer the police need us for.'

'Are you sure? We can get a hotel and see you tomorrow. I'd really be more comfortable if–'

'No, seriously, Dad, trust me. It's better this way. Stay there today. I'll keep you posted as I go and we'll see each other tomorrow. It's what I want.'

'OK ... if that's what you want. If you change your mind at any time, you let us know. Any time at all, Sarah. We love you.'

'Love you, too.'

As I hang up, Ashleigh's brother hands me an almond croissant. I wolf it down hungrily.

SURVIVAL GUIDE: THE MEDICAL EVIDENCE

Just think for a moment of all the random life-saving knowledge we know for improbable emergencies, often neatly packaged into catchy slogans. Growing up, we are taught to *Stop, drop and roll* if you catch fire, to react FAST (Face, Arms, Speech, Time) in case of a stroke. We know the Heimlich manoeuvre if someone is choking, and that someone in a drowning incident needs mouth-to-mouth resuscitation. From TV, we even know to play dead if a bear charges at us and to punch a shark in the nose if attacked. Yet, when was the last time you saw someone catch fire? Or drown? Why do we know this trivia about animals that are bordering on extinction? We teach these skills in the hope that we will never have to use them, but if the unthinkable did happen, they could save a life.

Contrast the fatalities for all those rare situations with the alarming numbers of people raped and sexually assaulted: in Ireland, 25% of Irish men and 42% of Irish women will experience rape or sexual violence in their lifetime.[4] Worldwide, that jumps up to an estimated 736 million women, or one in three women.[5] There are wild beasts much closer to home that are, regrettably, the opposite of near-extinction. Sexual predators roam our streets and proliferate in our society. But perplexingly, most of us don't know the first thing to do if we are raped, or someone we know is raped. These are the things we do not want to think about but that everybody should know in an emergency. We should be teaching everyone this stuff

4 The SAVI Report: *Sexual Abuse and Violence in Ireland, A national study of Irish experiences, beliefs and attitudes concerning sexual violence,* McGee. H., Garavan, R., de Barra, M., Byrne, J., Conroy, R. (Liffey Press, 2002).
5 World Health Organization, on behalf of the United Nations Inter-Agency Working Group on Violence Against Women Estimation and Data, 2021.

because it could genuinely save you or someone you know in future.

If you have been sexually assaulted or raped, you have just survived a horrific trauma, but the process of healing and taking your power back starts <u>right now.</u> The hours that follow the assault are critical. There are two things you need to start doing immediately: (1) preserve as much evidence as possible; and (2) kickstart your healing process by taking back your power and control.

Ask to be seen at a sexual assault treatment unit (SATU) immediately:
there are six SATUs in the Republic of Ireland: Cork, Dublin, Donegal, Galway, Mullingar and Waterford. You are most certainly exhausted, but it is crucial that you get evidence of the assault as soon as possible after it happens and, if at all possible, within 72 hours. DNA starts to disintegrate quickly after the assault. You will be safe and respected by the SATU staff. If you do pursue the case in court, the evidence gleaned by SATU will be crucial in terms of proof and conviction. You also don't have to go to SATU, you can go straight to any hospital or other rape clinic in the country.

Go to SATU before sleeping: it's incredibly important to go to SATU for treatment before going to sleep. As set out in Chapter 2, sleep interferes with memory and may affect your recall of the chain of events.

If you do not want to contact the gardaí, you don't have to: you can call SATU directly using the contact details displayed on their website (https://www2.hse.ie/sexual-assault-treatment-units/). They will provide you with a rape kit, a pregnancy test, anti-HIV medication and tend to any other injuries you have, for free.

Do not shower or wash (not even your face or hands) and do not brush your teeth or rinse your mouth: your skin is almost certainly crawling from coming into contact with your attacker and you are understandably desperate to get the creature who did this off you, but think about the DNA on your body. It is critical for evidence that any skin cells, blood, saliva, anything else that can prove who did this to you is collected by a forensic doctor. SATU will take swabs all over your body (including your face and hands). You will be able to shower and cleanse straight after the examination in SATU, if you wish.

Avoid going to the bathroom, if you can: this is to preserve any DNA, skin cells and other evidence from being lost. If you cannot avoid it, try to touch the area minimally (for example, gently pat rather than rub, etc).

Do not drink or eat anything, not even water, until the medical examination is complete: if this is not possible, for example if you have low blood sugar, try to eat or drink as little as possible. This will also help with avoiding going to the bathroom.

Do not brush your hair: SATU will comb through your hair for the perpetrator's skin cells.

Keep on the clothes you were wearing when the attack happened: if you need to put more clothes on, avoid skin-tight clothes. Be comfortable. If possible, use clothes you don't love because the gardaí will take them as evidence and it could be a long time before they are returned to you.

Once the examination is over, eat some sugar for the shock: even if you're not hungry, your blood-sugar will drop significantly, so at least try to drink a sugary soda or tea.

4.

Shadowland:
The After-effects of
Trauma

Diary entry, 18 July 2019:
'Everything outside feels surreal. Like a dream.'

The detective taking over the case, let's call her Ciara, comes to collect us from the hotel lobby and introduces herself. As the case involves a serious sexual offence it's been assigned to her department, which specialises in such crimes. She and another garda drive us from the hotel back to our apartment. Outside the flat, it's hard to get out of the car. *Where the hell is Bear when you need him?* Detective Ciara notices our hesitation and asks if we want them to come in with us. The three of us nod our heads furiously.

Walking into the apartment this time, in the cold light of day, feels like a horror movie. The air is heavy, and the hall sepulchral. Everywhere I look, I keep expecting to see Beast and his huge, angry eyes lurking in a corner, or hanging upside-down like something out of *The Exorcist*. The second garda patiently allows me to use him as a human shield as I guide him towards my bedroom, clutching his back and peering over his shoulder.

My room is a mess. The bed sheets and bedding have been ripped off and taken away by the forensics team, my poor plant is still sprawled across the carpet with the jagged shards of her broken pot, and a knocked-over lamp and various other items still litter the floor from the struggle. I stop in my tracks when I see the scuffle marks and blood on the wall near the door: a physical reminder of the fight that will haunt my nightmares for months to come. Examining it more closely, I take some satisfaction in noting that, from the direction of the spatter, none of it is my blood. That's all damage to Beast's hand inflicted by me. *Go, Sarah.* Slightly fearfully, I scan the floor for the chunk of his hand that I spat out, but luckily that too had been taken away by the police, along with the other evidence.

After the guards leave, the three of us go to pack our bags. The girls are going home and I'll be staying with a friend tonight. I've never been much of a scaredy cat, but right now I would rather chew broken glass than be in this place when night falls. I can't concentrate at all or think of what I need to take with me. Shoes? That seems important. A coat? It's mid-July. But what if I need to escape in the dead of night again? *What the hell have I put in this bag already?* Lack of concentration, including for simple or daily tasks, is a very common symptom of post-traumatic stress disorder (PTSD). We've all read articles on the COVID-19 brain fog – the mental fatigue and forgetfulness that set in due to months of lockdown and lack of social contact. Picture that, but on steroids. It will stay with me for months to come.

My inner OCD wants to tidy the room before we leave, but I am suddenly hit by a wave of exhaustion and need to sit down. We regroup in the living room and I collapse onto the sofa. Niamh suggests tea again. It turns out to be one of the most important things we did to reclaim the apartment. We all sat around the coffee table, sipping tea, the picture of normality.

'What time is it?'

'Eleven a.m.'

'Man, I'm exhausted.'

The girls' parents are due to come pick them up, but Niamh suggests we get something to eat first. Oh yeah, food. Bodies need that to function.

Ashleigh is frantically texting her friends and colleagues. I've asked her to tell my team that I will be indisposed for the day.

'Hey, Laura wants to come see you,' she says.

'There's no need. I'm fine.'

Laura is one of my best friends in work, but I can't deal with more people in this room right now.

'No, Sarah, she really wants to come see you.'

'I'm fine, really. I don't want to trouble her at work. She's got that deal closing.'

'OK, let me say this again – she is upset, Sarah. She *wants* to come and see you. Let her come.'

'Oh.' *I'm an idiot.* 'OK then, that's nice, thank you.'

'She's leaving now.'

Fifteen minutes later, Laura's eyes are huge as she walks in. I am afraid of her gaze. She is the first person unconnected to the assault to see me since I have been violated. I feel extremely exposed, like the ultimate walk of shame. I'm clutching one of the huge sofa pillows against me as some kind of armour.

'That *creature*,' she whispers, shaking her head softly as she sits down next to me.

Yep, creature will work too.

'I've been going with Beast.'

I don't know how to even begin to explain what happened, so I rip the Band-Aid off and get it over with in a few sentences. She's crying silently, too. *Why is everyone crying?* I still have not fully registered the immense significance of what was done to me. I hug the pillow in closer for comfort.

* * *

There's a quiet Italian restaurant a few streets down. As we step outside, everything feels surreal. Have you ever woken up from a dream and you think you're awake but actually you're in another dream? That's what this was like. I can't take anything in or connect to my surroundings. Looking at passing traffic, I am convinced that I could jump under a moving vehicle and come out of it perfectly unscathed. I also can't get over how calm I am. It's as though I have glided weightlessly into some sort of trance. This 'dream-like state', as it was later referred to by my therapist, was dissociation. This was the first symptom of the PTSD I experienced. Actually, my very first symptom was being triggered by the smell of cigarettes from the garda in our living room, but who's counting?

As we near the restaurant I'm walking stiffly, scanning the hands of every man we pass for a bite mark between the thumb and the index finger, looking for my rapist in the crowd. He could be anywhere, and I have no idea what he looks like. In the restaurant it's quiet enough, but the slightest unexpected noise sends my senses into a frenzy – the clatter of a fork dropping to the floor, a shout from the waiter, a door slamming. I jump every time someone walks behind me. I have this uncontrollable urge to constantly turn around and protect my back. That one is called hyperarousal, or hypervigilance, and it's another common response in the wake of trauma.

Hyperarousal is a lot less pleasant than dissociation, to put it mildly. Think of it as a constant state of extreme alertness, expecting the assault to happen again at any moment. In my case, hypervigilance tacked itself quite neatly on to dissociation, so I was either the most emotionless person on Earth, or ready to take on an attacker in a fight to the death: there was no in-between state.

After food, the girls go home and Laura takes me back to her place. I've always been grateful for my friends, but when you go through something like this, you truly relish the great friends. I have a memory blank as to what happened here. Too tired to stand, my next memory is of just sitting on the floor in Laura's bedroom. I couldn't tell you for how long. I can't even get up when another friend, Liana, comes by the flat that afternoon to check in on me.

Come night-time, I'm too afraid to sleep. Cue our next PTSD symptom: nightmares and insomnia. I'm afraid of allowing myself to become unconscious again. I'm terrified of what the nightmares will bring. I know Beast is still out there and I can't get it out of my head that he has followed us here somehow. I'm afraid I will roll over in my sleep and accidentally touch Laura, and the panic that would cause. Laura had selflessly offered to sleep on the sofa, but I'm also scared of being alone. Genius that she is, she fetches some cushions and builds a pillow fort between us so that we can sleep without touching. Relish the great friends, I tell you. Mercifully, I get some healing sleep.

* * *

The next day, Laura is going to work, so I am to go to Liana's for the day until my parents arrive. Laura gives me some cash and a spare wallet before I set off, and then it's me and my little overnight bag against the world. Walking into town is one of the most daunting things I have ever done. I'm hypervigilant again. There are so many *people*. There are people running, there are people shouting, there are people behind me. I skirt nervously around them, trying to put as much distance between them and me. It's like playing a little game called 'Don't feckin' touch Sarah'.

I need to buy a bus ticket to get to Liana's house, and it dawns on me that I should also get some paper to start recording names, dates and details of what has happened so far. (Once a lawyer, always a lawyer.) In the shop, my eyes land on a small black notebook. It reminds me of that evil little diary Tom Riddle used as a Horcrux in Harry Potter. *Perfect.* On the bus out of town, my body automatically gravitates towards the sides of the bus. I need to stand with my back to the wall. I'm keeping watch on everybody's movements and scanning their hands for any bite marks. Interestingly, I also notice that I'm much calmer around bigger guys than I am around men with a small build. My body instinctively tenses when I see a lanky man, particularly if he looks Spanish or Italian, which tells me that my subconscious has registered more of Beast's build than I can remember.

Liana's house is in a beautiful neighbourhood in south Dublin, and it's an oasis of peace when I arrive. The house is surrounded by a walled garden, climbing rosé bushes, and dotted with enchanting old glass window-panes that catch the morning light. Oh, and an absolute army of dogs. Her family helps rehabilitate rescue dogs before they can be adopted again. The front door swings open and I'm met by a stampede of happy Labradors and heart-stealing pups. They absolutely lose their minds any time someone comes in, and I'm no exception. Funnily enough, the swarm of dogs running and jumping around me doesn't trigger me at all. I always knew dogs had healing magic when it came to recovering from trauma, but I never realised the full power of that until just now. They sense emotions. When in dissociation, those big puppy eyes remind you to *feel*. One of them rests his head on my knee and looks up at me soulfully, while the youngest lab, Riley, is adamant on grabbing a mouthful of my long dress and gently pulling me into the garden to show me his toys. It's so healing to be able to touch another being and not flinch at the warmth of their skin.

The dogs are so protective and vigilant that for the first time I feel that I can let my guard down a little. They bark hysterically every time someone walks by the front gate, including two new gardaí who drop by later that afternoon for some follow-up questions. One of them introduces himself as my Family Liaison Officer (FLO). His name is John and he has been assigned to act as the middleman between me and the Garda investigation. He's very personable and his build is broad, so I'm not nervous in his presence. (Although that's possibly also because a couple of the dogs have decided to stay and stand guard between them and me.)

We sit in Liana's study and John explains that they have found my handbag. They need to take my fingerprints to eliminate them from those found by Forensics. I will have to go to the station for a follow-up statement as the team that took my initial statement don't specialise in sexual offences, and the Detective wants to make sure my evidence is as airtight as possible before submitting to the Director of Public Prosecutions (DPP). I mindlessly scratch the back of Riley's ear for comfort as I take

all this in. John then stands to hand me a list of victim support organisations, which he nervously draws back and slowly puts down on the table
when Riley emits a low warning growl. Bless little Riley.

* * *

After the gardaí leave, I try to rest on Liana's bed until my family arrive
from Galway. Thanks to the dogs, my hypervigilance is kept at bay, but no
matter how comfortable I am, wrapped in my warm blanket of dissociation, my eyes physically refuse to close. They just stare at the wall, almost
unblinking. I'm dreading the arrival of my parents. Up until now I've been
in a state of shock, but I can sense things are about to get incredibly emotional. I also feel a degree of shame at the thought of them seeing me. Some
niggling voice in the back of my mind keeps telling me that somehow, the
fact that I was defiled in that way makes me 'lesser' or 'unworthy', whatever
the hell that means.

It's uncomfortable when they arrive. As with Laura, I struggle to meet
their gaze. I don't want to see in their eyes how broken I am. We're usually
a tightknit and affectionate family, but I can feel these walls that have shot
up between us and I have no idea how to break them down. They're clearly
unsure how to react. It's awkward.

We're staying at my aunt's house in Wicklow, and during the drive down
there my state of calm has been traded in for totally erratic behaviour. I am
hyper. Words are tumbling out of my mouth faster than my money at a pub.
I'm jumping from one thought to another, almost joking to brush off the
severity of the attack. I can't tell them about the violation. I just can't do
that to them. I give them the 'vanilla' version, not mentioning the violation

and downplaying the violence of it like it's a badge of honour. They laugh along nervously, but then my dad says something amazing.

'He picked the *wrong* girl to mess with.'

All of a sudden my niggling shame has a streak of pride to keep her company.

* * *

That evening, I get a taste of my next PTSD symptom: my first panic attack. It's a bad one, not that there is any such thing as a 'good' panic attack.

As my family starts to relax a little that evening and digs into the wine, my mom's French nature is rearing its head. Physical affection is the cornerstone of all French *mamans*. She wants to hug her daughter, touch her hand, comfort her. It's the only way she knows how. She doesn't know yet that I cannot bear the thought of being touched. Every time she reaches out to touch me, I back away. Over the course of the evening there are less and less places to back into. I find myself building a fort of furniture, scattering chairs between myself and her like a barricade and retreating to the far corner of the dining table. She's not getting the subtle cues and keeps trying to come closer. I haven't noticed that I've been softly hyperventilating under my breath for a few minutes now, or that my hands are trembling under the table.

My dad has noticed, and he keeps trying to gently pull her hand away, but to no avail. I feel like I'm losing all control. I can't hear them speak over the sound of my pounding heart. She tries to reach over the table again and an overwhelming sense of fear sets it. I can't breathe. It's so intense I see blinking white lights. I want to run for my life, but I'm trapped inside my furniture fort. I completely break down and weep uncontrollably. It's impossible to speak through the heavy sobs. My still-shaking hands are clenched into fists and held up in front of my throat as protection, my whole spine has curled down into a defensive position. As the panic eventually subsides, I look up. My mother is crying, too. She doesn't understand my reaction. How could she? She has no idea I was violated. It shatters my heart to see hers break.

All I can do is repeat between sobs, 'I'm sorry. I'm sorry. I'm sorry.'

* * *

The next few days are a blur. My boss and friends send flowers to the house. Some brave friends face their fear of not knowing what to say and drop by to check in on me. Every outing is exhausting, but I make a point of swinging by the apartment with my family each day to start reclaiming it. The first day, we just sit for ten minutes and have a cup of tea. The next, I make myself take a shower in my bathroom. The day after, we buy new bedding and a new plant and tidy up the room. I even lie down on the bed for a couple of minutes and just breathe there slowly. I am so drained coming back to my aunt's home every day and yet I cannot find sleep at night. I need my sister, Alison, to sleep in the room with me, but the slightest sound sets me into full hyper-alert mode. Even the sound of her breathing is triggering.

We have to go to the Garda station for my follow-up statement and photos. That process is gruelling, even though the gardaí try to make it as comfortable as possible. I'm told I can bring someone with me, but when I suggest my dad, they take me aside and gently explain the sobering level of intimate detail we're about to run through. I ask him to wait outside with Alison instead.

I'm in the station for nearly four hours, but come the trial eighteen months later, I realise the immeasurable value of that second statement. Detective Ciara is one impressive lady, and goes through every single line of my original statement, adding clarifications wherever needed into the second statement. My evidence is now iron-clad.

'I know this is hard to talk about, but don't worry, I've heard it all. Nothing can shock me. It's critical we get the details as precise as possible for the trial, so they can't dispute something because it's "unclear". OK?'

'OK.'

'Alright, so in your statement you say, "he rammed his fingers inside of me". I know this is painfully obvious, but just to be crystal clear, what do you mean by that?'

'He penetrated me with his fingers.'

'He penetrated what?'

Ugh. 'My vagina.'

'And when you say it was violent, what do you mean?'

I pause to think about this one. 'Well, it hurt like hell, for one. I also bled for two days after. I still am. I have the blood-stained underwear to prove it.'

'Can we come pick those up from you as evidence?'

'Fine.'

'And when you say he strangled you, can you give more detail on that? What did he do exactly?'

As a Frenchie who loves to speak with her hands, I find it hard to explain without mimicking the movement. Pity they can't do a live drawing.

'He had both hands wrapped around my throat. He squeezed extremely hard – to the point where I couldn't breathe at all. The second time he strangled me, it was even harder. He was leaning his entire weight down onto his hands. It was crushing my throat. I still have the bruising on my neck from it.'

'We'll take photos of those bruises, and all injuries that aren't anywhere intimate. They'll form part of the Book of Evidence we give to the DPP.'

'And then?'

'Then the DPP decides if there is sufficient evidence to prosecute.'

The forensic photographer is thorough and gentle. We get the bruising on my neck and arms, the cut on my lip, my cut knees. Afterwards, Detective Ciara nods sympathetically.

'Well done, Sarah. This is great evidence, you did great. I know that can't have been very nice for you.'

I shrug apathetically. 'I've seen worse.'

That'll be my answer to everything from now on.

* * *

Above I have described some of the psychological effects of post-traumatic stress disorder (PTSD) that can happen in the aftermath of rape or sexual assault. I want to explain them in greater detail now, so you can clearly identify the symptoms and get a better handle on addressing them. However, it's important for me to strike a balance here. As a society, we have a responsibility to educate ourselves as to what survivors are going through, but I don't want to paint a harrowing picture which scares people off either. The last thing I want to do is to encourage the ignorant stereotype of a rape victim as the sad, broken shell of a woman, wailing and rocking in some corner in the foetal position, or gloomily haunting the shadows with a black veil drawn over her face. That's not what happens at all. In fact, in my own case, I was so worried that someone would uncover my dark secret and brand me with that cliché that I stayed extremely functional, to the point where very few people knew what had happened because most of the time I seemed so 'normal'. I want you to understand that you can be a rape victim and still experience moments of normality, even laughter, in the days and weeks that follow that trauma. Your life may have been turned upside-down, but that does not mean it is over. PTSD does not have to be permanent, and you will not be in its grips all of the time.

I also want to talk about this because the world over, but in Ireland especially, we struggle to talk about mental health. We refuse to speak openly about serious mental health issues for fear of saying the wrong thing, or out of some delusional machismo that we can never show weakness. But who is the stronger individual, the person who is incapable of acknowledging vulnerability, or the one who can bare it for all to see? We are so uneducated as to what survivors go through because heaven forbid we have to imagine for even two minutes what walking through that kind of fire can be like. And it's not just rape or sexual violence victims who experience life-changing PTSD. The majority of people will go through grief, loss or other trauma that will trigger very similar symptoms. We all have a duty to break the silence, because survivors should never have to suffer alone.

A little disclaimer here: I am (obviously) not a medical expert. The things I talk about in this book are things I have discovered through trial and error, through a lot of research to understand what I was going through, and through nuggets I have from my yoga and mindfulness practice. These are my own musings based on *my* experience. This is how it happened to me.

What I want you to take from this is that you are capable of healing. No two healing journeys are the same. Their only common denominator is that they are not linear. There will be great days and there will be days when you want to hide under the bed covers. You might surprise yourself how fine you feel for weeks before you feel triggered, or how quickly you recover and then get a major setback. As unique as your trauma was, so will your recovery be.

That said, dear reader, I understand that this is a heavy chapter. You've taken the first step in showing up, but you also need to be mindful of yourself and know when to reserve your headspace. This might not be the right time to explore this chapter, so read at your leisure and be kind to yourself.

* * *

Post-traumatic stress disorder, or PTSD, is a mental disorder triggered by a traumatic event. It manifests in a huge range of symptoms, but you won't go through all of them, nor feel them all at the same time, nor all the time for that matter. We hear the word 'PTSD' used often, but it's hard to capture its full spectrum.

PTSD affects the dynamic between the amygdala and the prefrontal cortex. The amygdala is the 'alarm' part of your brain, which is highly alert to threats and is responsible for triggering the 'fight or flight' response. The prefrontal cortex rules our rational decision-making. Normally, the prefrontal cortex regulates the amygdala by assessing the overall situation, instead of jumping to a frenzy at the first sign of alarm. With PTSD, however, the amygdala goes into overdrive, hijacking the prefrontal cortex and preventing it from rationalising our emotions or impulses. In short – you're jumpy and too alert to be able to focus on the non-life-threatening Word document you're trying to edit. In the months that followed the attack, I often found myself in a daze or struggling to focus. I worried a lot about losing my job because, in fairness, confusion and absentmindedness are not exactly top qualities you want in your lawyer.

If you have suffered a trauma or experience PTSD, I think it is empowering to be able to identify those symptoms and put words on what you're going through. The very wide range of potential PTSD symptoms can be categorised under three main headings: (1) Re-experiencing the trauma, (2) Avoiding the trauma (or the processing of it), and (3) Hyper-alertness (also called hyperarousal and hypervigilance).

Re-experiencing	Avoiding	Hyperarousal
• Nightmares	• Dissociation	• Extreme alertness
• Flashbacks	• Memory loss or gaps	• Panic attacks
• Intrusive and/or distressing thoughts and images	• 'Blanking out' mid-conversation	• Expecting the trauma to happen again
• Being triggered by memories or senses connected to the trauma	• Inability to concentrate, confusion, forgetfulness or absentmindedness	• Intolerance or aversion to certain smells, noises or other sensory triggers
• Trembling or shaking hands	• Withdrawing (from life, friends, hobbies, etc.)	• Being jumpy or easily startled
• Pain or pressure in the body from the trauma	• Depression	• Erratic or manic behaviour
• Chest tightness	• Insomnia / Sleep disorders	• Obsessive compulsive behaviour, e.g. constantly checking doors are locked
• Migraines and headaches	• Suicidal thoughts	
	• Self-harm	

• Nausea	• Substance abuse	• Phobias
• Dizziness	• Grief	• Anxiety
• Hyperventilating		• Anger, irritability, hostility or aggression
		• Elevated heart rate

I would never tell someone what to do, but my two cents' worth, if they're useful, is that as this is a mental disorder, it is a lot to take on without professional help. I'd highly recommend at least considering therapy, more particularly specialised counselling for sexual violence trauma and/or PTSD.

Now, before I continue, and I'll go deeper into this in Chapters 5 and 10, I think it's important for me to pause here and say a few words on the perilous risk that survivors are at in Ireland due to our Neanderthal laws. Irish case law developed about twenty to thirty years ago allows counselling records of a rape or sexual assault victim to be disclosed as evidence in trial. The sole purpose of this practice is to poke holes in the *victim's* evidence, any reinforcement it brings to the Prosecution's case has no bearing on the trial whatsoever. The Prosecution team, Defence team *and the accused* all get to read your deepest, darkest thoughts, all of them voiced in a place that you thought was of the utmost confidence, privacy and trust. Barbaric.

I cannot describe the panic and agony when I was told, nearly five months later, that this would happen, and not only that, but my therapist had also taken detailed notes of our weekly sessions. There is a process requiring the victim to consent to this[6] but, to cut a long story short, if you do not consent, Defence can still ask that the judge force the release of the therapy notes. Supposedly, Prosecution redacts anything 'not relevant' to the assault, but as

6 Under section 19A of the Criminal Evidence Act 1992, as inserted by section 39 of the Criminal Law (Sexual Offences) Act 2017.

Defence can challenge the redaction and you don't get to see what has been redacted, who knows what is actually being disclosed? This inhumane practice has deterred countless rape and sexual assault victims from getting the professional help they desperately need, sometimes for years on end, because they do not want their abuser to read their notes or their records to be used against them at trial.

All I'll say is that you can discuss with your therapist or counsellor, ahead of or at your appointment, the ground rules around their note-taking. You can ask them to take little to no notes, or to avoid recording certain aspects (for example, if you don't want it known that you are adopted, or that you were raped before). Certain places in Ireland already do this because they know about this moronic law, but always ask ahead to be sure. I would recommend, however, that the counsellor does take down a record of dates and times you attended and, if possible, a very short note to prove you were impacted (for example, 'Patient is suffering from serious PTSD due to the assault. Ran through some calming exercises to help with panic attacks.'). They don't play fair? We won't either. Fight fire with fire.

That dinosaur of a practice aside, each person's PTSD experience will be unique. In mine, one of the dominating features that took over my life was dissociation. The period that followed the attack was a complete blur. If you had told me those months only lasted a couple of days, or a couple of years, I would have believed you. The laws of time no longer moved in one linear direction. I was trapped, frozen in the night of the break-in. Any past before that seemed as though it had never existed, and any future ahead no longer mattered. Dissociation was the Shadowland – this place of desolation that I had floated into, halfway between the land of the living and the land of the dead, completely alone.

To be honest with you, dissociation wasn't all unpleasant. All of my senses became numbed, sensations of pain or cold were dulled, food didn't have much taste, and anything I looked at seemed two-dimensional, like the screen of a video-game. I was completely disconnected from everything. My body no longer felt like my own. Instead, I became the keeper of this physical vessel and I was vaguely aware that I had to do certain things to keep the motor running, like breathe in and out, drink water, let it rest and eat something occasionally. I remember lying down on my bed at times and looking up at my hands thinking, *this is so weird*, trying to register that they were actually mine.

On the flip side, however, the state of disconnection was so deep that everything was an effort, even breathing. I wanted to do nothing but sit there and just exist. Not even exist, actually. After each exhale, I came to such a long pause that I wondered if I'd ever take another breath in again, if it would even be worth the exertion. That stillness in the body after the last of the air had left my lungs was so blissfully soft that I dreamt of slipping into sweet unconsciousness and never waking up again.

Whether you realise it or not, you have experienced mild dissociation before – it happens to all of us when we forget ourselves while daydreaming or get lost in a captivating book. Dissociation is the temporary disconnection from our sense of self, our memories or perception of our surroundings. More intense dissociation is very common with PTSD, where the trauma is just too overwhelming for our small human minds to comprehend. It is one of the brain's many coping strategies to help distance us from what happened: a mental escape hatch, if you will. In its severest form, dissociation can manifest as de-personalisation (the splintering of identity into separate personalities) or, as in my case, total detachment from the present moment, as though nothing I was experiencing was real.

Dissociation also often causes memory loss or gaps, sometimes to the point of being incapable of remembering important personal information about yourself. I find it interesting to go back to the basic science on this one. Memories are created in three stages – encoding, storage and retrieval. At the encoding stage, the information gathered from all of your different senses (sight, touch, hearing, etc.) is converted by the hippocampus – the part of your brain responsible for learning and memory formation – into a structure that can be saved down (storage) and recalled as long-term memories (retrieval). With a highly traumatic event, however, the sensations and emotions gathered during the event can be too overwhelming for the hippocampus to process. Think of it as a computer crashing when processing a file that is too large. Instead, the brain will fragment the memory so that it can encode it, which leads to irregularities in the episodic structure of that memory. In other words, the narrative has gaps and errors because the real narrative is too distressing for the brain to store and retrieve as a whole.

For me, this led to entire periods of time disappearing from my recollection – not just of the attack itself but also of the weeks that followed. To this day, I am incapable of telling you how I got from my apartment to Laura's house, or what I did until my parents arrived the next day. This highlights again the importance of giving your statement to the gardaí as soon as possible after the assault. Even twelve hours after the break-in, the details and sequence of that night were already starting to blur in my mind.

The most striking thing about dissociation is how strong the sense of disconnection is. It's hard to describe. Nothing around me mattered anymore. I felt absolutely nothing. No joy, no pain, no panic, no hope, no sadness. Nothing. It was like all of my emotions had been powered down. As a person who normally feels things very strongly, this was difficult territory for me. Usually, the smallest of simple pleasures will send me off on a gratitude high, and an emotional song can have me watery eyed in seconds. Yet here I was, a stranger to myself, feeling nothing at all. Through time and effort, I would find and embrace all my emotions again (see Chapter 10).

The only thing that pulled me out of this dissociative state was moments of hypervigilance, triggered by loud noises or touch, which often culminated in panic attacks if the trigger was not diffused immediately. Hypervigilance translates into very physical symptoms – being easily startled or scared, restlessness and panic attacks, trembling, even severe social anxiety and outbursts of anger or tears. You see danger everywhere, even in safe settings. I remember having to walk between two male colleagues chatting away in a corridor and trembling because of the irrational fear that one of them would try to reach out and touch me. Five months after the attack, I broke into a full-blown panic attack one evening because my mother absentmindedly stroked my hand over some lovely Christmas cocktails.

Those symptoms subsided after a number of months but would come back in certain situations. In the lead-up to the trial, a year-and-a-half later, it came back with such a vengeance that I would get triggered by the sound of breathing or the most random smells, such as perfume or even kale (don't ask me why, I still don't know). One panic attack was so severe it translated into temporary blindness. I literally lost my sight, similar to a head rush when you stand up too fast, except it lasted for an hour. After it subsided, there was a big gaping hole in the middle of my visual field and I could only see out of my peripheral vision for hours (and with a plane to catch that afternoon, talk about stressful).

What helped me through those first weeks and months was journaling. I made a point of it. Initially, it was hard. I've never been one to keep a diary.

The blank page just looked up at me uncooperatively. But I was determined. *Right, lawyer mode.* I started with the dates and the times. Then the names. I stuck to a bullet-point list and wrote down names of the gardaí, the SATU staff, the Garda station and the hotel where we waited, the medication I was given. I then started retracing my steps and wrote down excerpts of conversations with my flatmates, the gardaí and the doctors. I recorded every panic attack, every flashback, every nightmare.

That was all the practical stuff covered. Harder were the feelings I was experiencing. Flicking back through the blackened pages now, on some of them my pen has pierced through the page from anger. I don't revisit them often, but having a record of how I felt day-by-day proved invaluable, not just when I gave evidence at the trial, but also in identifying the obstacles to my healing.

So, that's all a lot to take in. Believe me, it was a lot to live with. My key takeaway from it is that this is completely new territory. Until you have experienced PTSD, there is nothing that can prepare you for it, so approach it with no expectations and an open mind bordering on curiosity. Observe yourself without judgement. Your journey will not follow mine. It will be unique to you and that's OK. Be kind and patient with yourself. It takes time. PTSD is a coping mechanism, designed to help you survive your trauma, but you will leave the Shadowland again.

SURVIVAL GUIDE: THE AFTER-EFFECTS OF TRAUMA

The information here is pulled from what I have learnt through my own experience, through personal research and through stories that other survivors and therapists have shared with me. The crucial thing to remember is that although PTSD may hijack your mind and body for a time, it is not you, it does not last forever and there are very effective treatments for it. You can and will get through this, at your own pace.

Understand post-traumatic stress disorder: PTSD is a natural consequence of trauma. Essentially, your brain has not registered that the danger is over, so your body continues to try to defend you long after the threat has passed. PTSD manifests in many different forms, all of them designed to keep you alert and ready to respond to a potential threat. The main symptoms are set out above, on pages 86-87, so you know what to watch out for and also to put words on what you are dealing with. If you want to read up more on it, I'd recommend you start with the Mayo Clinic's page on PTSD (www.mayoclinic.org/syc-20355967) or the book that is the bible on the matter, *The Body Keeps the Score* by Bessel van der Kolk.

The four trauma responses: fight, flight, freeze or fawn (see Chapter 1), are often carried on into the PTSD phase. Your mind is stuck on the trauma and is therefore likely to recreate patterns from it. This is not your fault, but it can be helpful to you if you can identify the patterns and talk them through with a friend or therapist. (See also Get Professional Help, below.)

Have no expectations: approach your PTSD with an attitude close to curiosity. Every single survivor is different, and your PTSD will be unique to you. Watch, observe and accept what comes. I promise you that this too will pass. Trust yourself.

Your pace is the right pace: with trauma, there is no right or wrong pace. Your trauma is still valid, no matter how you react to it. There will be peaks and troughs, good days and bad days. Take it one day, one hour at a time. Just keep going, warrior.

Rest and give yourself time: you might feel fine for a long time after the assault. It is completely fine if you do. But you have been through an incredibly traumatic event, so you need to let the dust settle for a while and be kind to yourself during that time.

Be vocal about how you're feeling: dealing with PTSD is one of the hardest things to do, and it can be easy for people around you to forget what you're going through. Don't be afraid to remind them of how you're feeling, or to communicate your needs and boundaries to them.

Be prepared to stand up for yourself: bring someone with you to all medical appointments and to the Garda station. You would hope that people will be compassionate, and most of them are, but unfortunately there are idiots everywhere. You will need someone who doesn't feel fragile to stand up for you when you are too exhausted to do it for yourself.

Put pen to paper: start recording things that are happening and ideally in one place, like a diary. I know it can be painful at first to write it all down, but it is important, particularly if you're experiencing dissociation or memory loss. Tracking your progress will help your recovery, and some details could be crucial if you go to trial. One of the deciding factors in my case was the amount of detail I gave in my evidence, because it made me such a credible witness. I would not have remembered that evidence without all my contemporaneous notes. So much of a rape trial is based on 'your word against his', so write down every PTSD symptom, record dates, names and examples. The more detail, the better. List it in bullet-points, if you have to, but get it all down on paper.

Seek animal company: if you don't have a pet, ask a friend if you can walk their dog, spend an hour with their cat, or even volunteer at your local DSPCA or animal rescue centre. Pet companionship offers next-level healing, they keep us present, remind us to feel emotions and even activate our brain to release endorphins and dopamine.

Breathe your way through panic attacks: I get asked often how to deal with panic attacks. While there is no magical solution to stop a panic attack, there are a few techniques that have helped me, and they all focus on the breath. Breath is king, it can reduce stress and anxiety by regulating the nervous system, particularly if you focus on lengthening your exhale. Try some basic breathing techniques and you will soon feel the benefits. *Box breathing* is inhaling for four seconds, holding for four seconds, exhaling for four seconds, holding for four seconds, and repeat.

If you are feeling very panicked, try two sharp inhales through the nose, followed by one long, slow exhale through the mouth. Do that three to five times and see if it helps. Another great one to regulate the nervous system when feeling anxious generally is the *4-7-8 technique:* breathe in for four counts, hold in for seven counts, breathe out slowly for eight counts – and repeat that pattern for a minute or two. (More breathing techniques are listed in the Survival Guide at the end of Chapter 5.)

Get professional help: no matter how strong you are, you need help on this one. Acknowledging that is not weakness, it is strength. Friends and family can help you, but only up to a level. Therapy worked for me, however not everyone finds it beneficial. An Garda have a Victims Information Leaflet with a list of support organisations for victims of crime (https://www.garda.ie/en/victim-services/). There are online self-directed courses, including the DRCC's 'Moving Forward' online support programme. You can also look at their Coping Resources (www.drcc.ie/support/coping-resources/). If you do want to explore therapy, there are many techniques to help you overcome PTSD and you can discuss your options with your therapist and identify which would suit you best. The most common ones are:

- **Cognitive-Behavioural Therapy (CBT):** a conversation-based approach that explores and challenges behaviour patterns or traumatic memories and develops healthier ways to cope with PTSD.
- **Dialectical Behaviour Therapy (DBT):** a combination of strategies like mindfulness and acceptance to help people understand their triggers and develop healthier responses. Often used to treat self-harm, personality or mood disorders and substance abuse.

- **Eye Movement Desensitisation and Reprocessing (EMDR):**
  guided eye movements to help the brain 'reset' and process emotional
  trauma. This is a very effective way to deal with nightmares, flashbacks, or panic attacks.

Protect your counselling records: a heartbreaking number of survivors
do not seek therapy in Ireland for fear that their counselling records
will be seized by the Defence in a trial. It is true that the Defence can
request your therapist's notes, and often without your consent, but now
that you know this, you can put the necessary safeguards in place. You
can phone your therapist in advance and discuss with them the dangers
of record-taking and the level at which you ar comfortable they take
notes. Ideally, they should record at least dates and times when you
attend, to show that you required ongoing therapy, and they could also
note the broad outline of your visits – for example: 'Patient is suffering
from PTSD. Completed exercises to deal with panic attacks'. For further
information on this, you can contact the 24/7 Dublin Rape Crisis Centre
helpline, which is anonymous: 1800 77 8888 and www.drcc.ie. Before
agreeing to anything regarding your counselling records, even just with
the DPP, you should also get _free_ legal aid from the Legal Aid Board
(www.legalaidboard.ie) to make sure you are not accidentally waiving
your right to non-disclosure for trial.

Invest in your healing: it is never too soon to start focusing on your
recovery. While healing won't be linear, it's good to get into a discipline
of it early on. Look up the Survival Guide at Chapter 10 in your own
time for some pointers on where to start.

5.

Fire: Anger

Diary entry, 20 November 2019:
'I'm so fucking angry. I have never felt rage of this magnitude.
I'm trying so hard to be at peace with what's happened, but it
is exhausting to have to keep forgiving the same disappointing
people and behaviours.'

It is no exaggeration to say that trauma like this strikes to the very foundations of a person's psyche. It rocked the most fundamental pillars of my existence – my sense of safety, my relationships with family and friends, even my sense of identity. I still remember stepping out of that shower in the sexual assault unit and looking into the mirror, thinking I would never come back from this. I lived in fear that I would forever be branded as a rape victim, the untouchable who people speak in whispers around and are uncomfortable making eye contact with. Trauma of this magnitude, it blows a hole sideways through every dimension of your life. It is a volcano, destroying everything in its path and freezing you in time like the preserved bodies of Pompeii. After the night of the attack, my life as I knew it felt as though it had been reduced to ashes.

You know what comes out of ash? Goddamn phoenixes. Did you also know that volcanic ash is one of the most fertile types of soil on the planet? It contains vital plant nutrients, such as potassium and phosphorus, and dozens of minerals, including magnesium, iron, calcium and zinc, which all contribute to plant growth. Because of the high quantities of carbon it traps, it increases overall ground fertility. Once that ash comes in contact with earth and water, it slowly releases these minerals and nutrients over time, allowing seeds and plants to grow like (pardon the pun) wildfire.

Ash is not a bad thing. Sometimes ash, which often symbolises a form of finality, can be the presage of new beginnings, if you put the work in. It can be an opportunity to replant, to rebuild and to regrow a flourishing garden that will blossom more beautifully than the one that burned down before it. So, if ash is not the toxic element that we perceive it to be, then what is? Well, there's that old myth from the Third Punic War in 146 BC, when the Romans captured and destroyed the mighty city of Carthage, turning Africa into the latest province of the Roman Empire. After sacking and burning the Carthaginian stronghold to the ground, legend has it that the Romans, in vengeful hatred of the Phoenicians' defiance, sowed the ash-covered earth with salt so that nothing could ever grow from it again. The salt is what you need to watch out for, not the ash.

Salt is toxic. It corrodes almost all materials and weakens even the strongest of metals. In your life, salt will manifest in many forms – toxic friendships, toxic environments, toxic thoughts – and they all prevent you from healing. The problem is that sodium, the toxic chemical element in salt, is found in almost everything (even ash), and so it is impossible to avoid completely. But during your healing, you need to limit the concentrations of salt to which you are exposed to as low dosages as humanly possible.

Anger is the greatest salt of them all. It burns through your heart like salt rubbed into an open wound. As I left the Shadowland behind and started returning to the land of the living, all that numbness began slowly morphing into towering rage over how little was left in the ashes of my old life, or how few people seemed to be affected by my time of exile in the shadows.

The first spark that set me ablaze, however, was my visit to another hospital a few days after attending SATU, by far the worst experience in the days that followed the assault.

As part of my treatment in SATU, I was given a five-day course of Pre-Exposure Prophylaxis (PrEP) to reduce the risk of contracting HIV. The risk was relatively small, but as the open wound on Beast's hand had come into contact with the internal cut he had inflicted, there was still a risk. Therefore, I'm to consult with an infectious disease specialist to confirm whether I'll need the full month-long preventive treatment. I really hope that I don't need it because I already have extreme nausea and exhaustion from the medication. It's also been giving me agonising migraines, apparently a common side-effect of PrEP.

On the night of the attack, the wonderful nurse in SATU had reassured me on the process: 'Don't you worry, honey. They have a separate waiting room for sexual assault victims that you can wait in quietly. Just tell them you're referred by SATU and they'll take you there immediately.'

While the lifesaving angels of SATU would be a tough act to follow, I was still expecting some level of professionalism and compassion from this clinic on my arrival, three days later. The difference between the two was a chasm. Not ten seconds in, Alison, Dad and I are met by the crabbiest receptionist I have ever had the misfortune of meeting.

'Hi, I have an appointment with the doctor.' I lower my voice as I'm conscious of the busy waiting room. 'I've been referred in from SATU.'

She does not look up and waves towards the check-in docket. 'Take a number.'

'Oh, sorry, I'm referred in by SATU?'

'Take a number.'

'Um, sorry, but I was told by SATU that there might be a separate room I can wait in? I'm quite nervous around people, understandably.'

She looks up impatiently and snaps, 'Take. A. Number.'

I'm so taken aback by her rude tone, I don't even protest. I grab a ticket and fearfully cross the room to sit with my back to the wall. There are *so many* people, most of them men who smell like they haven't showered in a week. A couple of them are clearly drunk. One *reeks* of cigarettes and body odour. Another girl – clearly a minor – is here with her dad, pale as a ghost and looking absolutely petrified. I know why she's here and I am choking back tears for her. My dad and sister do their best to guard the chairs around me, to prevent anyone sitting too close. We wait for thirty minutes and I'm getting more and more restless. Every time the door slams my head jolts up.

And then it happens. A man walks in, wearing a prison jumpsuit, hands and feet chained together and escorted by four prison officers. He's probably here because he did something similar to what Beast did to me, if not worse.

Oh no. No no no no no *NO*. Panic attack number two descends within seconds. In your typical Irish not-wanting-to-make-a-scene fashion, however, this time I stay glued to my chair, crying silently and shaking uncontrollably.

'This can't be happening.'

Alison sees red. 'Screw this.'

She marches up to the receptionist.

'We have been waiting for half an hour. My sister was referred in by SATU. She's been through an incredibly traumatic assault and was told there would be somewhere quiet for her to wait. She is clearly in great distress, she was shown zero compassion and now there's a CONVICT sitting a few seats away. This is unacceptable.'

The sour receptionist waves vaguely towards the corridor. Alison eventually walks back to us, muttering some colourful language under her breath.

'They say you can wait in the corridor.'

Dad is concerned. 'Surely that's worse, Sarah? There are a lot of people coming and going.'

'Anywhere is better than here.'

I clutch my bag and sprint past the convict, holding my breath in case he smells of cigarettes, too. I wait another twenty minutes in the corridor before I am eventually called in.

I wait in the medical room for fifteen more minutes before the nurse and doctor finally walk in. Initially, I don't even realise *he's* the specialist. He does not say a word, does not look at me. He glares at the chart, mutters something to the nurse before leaving the chart on the table and walking out. I never see him again. Doctor Grouch it is. The nurse, God help her, is clueless. She asks moronic questions like, 'Why are you crying?' and, when I explain the assault through tears, 'Are you over it now?'

She then explains that there is a PrEP Protocol to decide whether the month-long course is required and that it covers every possible scenario, from bites and scratches to rape. Or so they thought. Turns out, the Protocol does not cover when the *victim* bites the attacker. Dr Grouch apparently scratched his head at that one for a while before taking the safer course of recommending the treatment. I am gleefully distracted from my distress for a moment and feel a defiant sense of pride. *That's right, she bites.* My bubble is swiftly burst by Clueless Nurse stabbing me multiple times in the arm with a needle before she can find a vein to take the blood samples. I'm told I'll have to come back in periodically over a period of five months, because that's how long HIV can take to be detected. They'll continue taking samples and running tests every few weeks until then. *Wonderful.*

I'm shaken for days after that incident. It shocks me that medical professionals can treat vulnerable crime victims with so little humanity. I think of that young girl and her dad and I wonder about the 47% of victims reporting abuse in Ireland who have never told anyone, and so have had to come through these corridors alone.[7] And that's just those who actually report. I'm starting to see more clearly why so few do.

* * *

Anger is a perfectly natural emotion, especially after an ordeal as traumatic as a rape or sexual assault. Without anger, we would not be experiencing the full range that life has to offer. Anger is also highly useful. Unlike the 'low energy' emotions, like sadness or worry, it motivates you to *do* things, even if those things are punching walls. When channelled in the right way, anger can be a vector for your healing and spur you on to do great things. I used to take to HIIT workouts with an absolute vengeance every time

---

7 The SAVI Report: *Sexual Abuse and Violence in Ireland, A national study of Irish experiences, beliefs and attitudes concerning sexual violence,* McGee. H., Garavan, R., de Barra, M., Byrne, J., Conroy, R. (Liffey Press, 2002). Despite government announcements that this 2002 report was to be updated by mid-2020, it is still pending renewal as at the date of publication. This is the figure quoted by the DRCC in 2020.

my rage started bubbling up – and baby, guess who got herself some abs? Anger is ultimately the reason I decided to go public about my experience. I was enraged at how appallingly our self-proclaimed 'victim-friendly' justice system could treat rape victims, and I wielded that rage like a weapon in calling for change (more on that in Chapter 9).

The problem with anger is not the emotion itself, but the holding on to it. Imagine you are holding a searing hot stone. You might be able to keep it in your hand for a few seconds unscathed, but you are going to get burned if you hold on to it much longer. Even after the heat dissipates and the stone becomes cool, if you continue to hold on to it for hours, the muscles in your arm will tire and cramp up, before eventually becoming paralysed. Long-term anger makes for bitter people, and bitter people are debilitated by the weight of their own resentment. They call it 'carrying' a grudge for a reason. To quote a line attributed to many different authors, holding onto anger is like drinking poison and expecting the other person to die. The only person who is going to get hurt is you. It does not matter how many seeds of joy you plant in those ashes or how meticulously you tend those shoots, if you cling onto your anger, it will poison the earth and dissolve all of your hard work.

The flip side of this is that avoiding anger can be just as harmful as holding on to it. If you go about your day, as so many of us do, on 'autopilot', unaware of what you are feeling, you will miss the first signs of anger trying to call for your attention. And if you continue to repress or ignore the emotion, it is going to compound, much like grief or anxiety. Naturally, we don't want to feel these emotions. They are highly unpleasant, to say the least. But they are there for a reason. They are usually trying to tell you something. And the harder you push them down, the harder they will punch back.

I've chosen to address anger as its own chapter because in my journey, it was my Everest. It's no coincidence that it features in the middle of this book, because it was the peak of the mountain that I thought I would never conquer. Each survivor is different, each person will have their own monster to tackle – be it depression, anxiety, guilt or grief to name but a few. And, to be clear, I'm distinguishing here between the *emotions* of being depressed or anxious, which are temporary, and the *states* of depression or anxiety, which are longer-term, pathological conditions. For me, the monster was anger. I can only speak to my own experience, but from listening to many survivors, it became clear to me that these different demons have a lot in common, including how deeply they roam within us and also how they can be tamed.

Anger was my Everest because it was not a state with which I was familiar. I am not an angry person. If anything, I'm much more familiar with the low-energy 'negative' states, including a couple of encounters with depression. As hard as depression is, that is territory I know and have some sense of how to manage if and when it reappears. Anger, on the other hand, was new to me. Through my yoga practice, I had developed a good discipline of letting things go and not sweating the small stuff. Sure, like everyone, there are things that grind my gears, but nothing that a heavy sigh and a wee kick-boxing session can't cure. That is not something you can do when dealing with rage of this intensity. There is no rant in the world that can lift even a fraction of this weight that is crushing down on your chest. Anger is something I struggled with so fundamentally, it came very close to being my undoing.

There is no straightforward formula with emotions on this scale. It's true that time is a great healer, but time doesn't feel like it's on your side when you feel stuck in it. You are going to need a great deal of support and self-compassion to work through this. That is why I want to share here some of the insights I found along the journey, because I wish someone had said them to me at the start of mine.

* * *

Naive as I was, I thought I had escaped anger altogether. I did not feel it for a very long time. My healing process was coming along nicely – I went to counselling, did my yoga, avoided the salt, replanted in the ash and tended the new-grown shoots. In the months that followed the assault, people would ask me how I managed to be so calm and positive. The answer was always a smile and: 'It's the yoga'. *I'm a yoga teacher*, I thought, *I practice compassion and gratitude and acceptance, I have managed to miraculously dodge anger through this practice.* Fool.

I did not notice the anger slowly creeping up on me over that year. It was almost unnoticeable at first. It started as impatience, which I was already prone to pre-assault. I am not exactly a patient woman. I love getting stuff done and checked off my to-do list. But then the impatience started to turn into irritability. More eye-rolls per day than you could count. Deep, frustrated sighs. Waking up to my Fitbit displaying an alarmingly elevated heartrate. Getting exceedingly annoyed at printers not working and slamming on the keyboard when writing emails. I did not notice how resentful I had started to become.

My anger had been bottled up, and it wasn't directed only at Beast, but at an endless list of people. Doctor Grouch and that hostile receptionist who denied me all dignity. The close friends who abandoned me at a time when I needed them most. Work pushing me so hard despite what I was going through. The nonsensical inefficiencies and unfairness of our broken criminal justice system. My family, who kept forgetting about my aversion to being touched. The irresponsibility of the media when reporting on sexual assault and rape. The news articles that later stole my coming out from me. The racism every time I told my story and the first question out of people's mouths was, 'Was he foreign?', as if that somehow explained away his senseless act.

I was angry when the gardaí rang, out of the blue, to tell me that my private therapy records would be taken as evidence for the trial and that if I refused, all it would achieve would be to delay the trial because the judge would force the release anyway (more on this below). I was angry at the lack of information out there for victims, and the fact that no matter how many questions I asked, I could never get a straightforward answer. I was angry at the fear in people's eyes when they looked at me, and how they started treating me differently. I was angry at how violence against women and rape culture are so normalised and rammed down our throats on a daily basis, from the Epstein judicial fiasco to the heinous murder of Sarah Everard. I was angry that no one could relate to what I was going through.

I was furious, and I had every right to be. I had to fight a battle I had asked for no part in. My old life was gone, and it was never coming back. I was not ready to grieve for it, nor leave it behind.

In fact, to be quite honest with you, for a long time one of the only people I was not mad at was Beast. The way my brain processed the attack, it was as though I had been mauled by a wild animal. If you are attacked by a boar, you can't be mad at the boar. It's just a feral animal in its wild state, it is not capable of malice. But on 19 November 2019, four months after the attack, the gardaí dropped by my office to give me the court summons for the trial and I saw his name for the first time. Beast had a name. Out of nowhere, it hit me – that's not an animal. That is a person. A person with a family, a mother and a father who chose that name for him. A person who, unlike a wild boar, has a consciousness and can understand the consequences of his actions. The nausea rose in waves as my eyes locked on those letters. Even now, I still refuse to acknowledge his name, almost as a way to deny him his humanity. To me he was Beast from the moment he committed the unspeakable. There was no redeeming his soul after that.

The flames of fury were fanned further when reading the charges on the summons – *aggravated sexual assault* and *aggravated burglary*. It felt strange, the night that had turned my life upside-down reduced to five words. My mind runs back to the excruciating hours of giving my statements, going into so much detail about how I thought I was going to die.

'But he tried to kill me. How is that not attempted murder?'

I was gently told by the gardaí that attempted murder was too hard to prove and that there was not enough evidence for the DPP to prosecute for that. My crestfallen face clearly made them feel sorry for me because they tried to comfort me.

'But the maximum sentence for aggravated sexual assault is the same as for rape. It's life imprisonment.'

'That's never given as a sentence for rape in Ireland, though.'

Uncomfortable silence. *Man*, they must hate dealing with a lawyer. I spare them the additional reminder that 'life' in Ireland only means twenty years, on average, so we're looking at a lot less for Beast. And that's before we factor in good behaviour.

'And all sentences run concurrently anyway, so the result would be the same,' I added bitterly.

They nodded.

That always struck me as a ludicrous rule in Irish law. If you commit more than one crime in a short space of time, the sentences you are given for each crime all run at the same time – meaning you will only really serve the longest sentence. There is no possibility for the judge to consider all the charges together and give one total sentence that is fair given all the circumstances. Granted, the US system is equally ridiculous in that you can tack on sentence after sentence until you reach a total of over 600 years' imprisonment. But there ought to be a middle ground. Otherwise, once you've raped someone, you might as well go rob a bank, assault bystanders to your heart's content and impersonate a dozen police officers because your maximum sentence will always be the same. There is zero incitement not to go on an absolute rampage.

Additionally, I found out later, much to my distress and astonishment, that in Ireland almost all sentences (except for life) are automatically reduced by 25% under Article 59 of the Prison Rules, 2007, in practice even without good behaviour. So in reality, you will only ever serve three-quarters of your sentence. And they have the audacity to say that our criminal justice system is victim-friendly. Honey, please.

I was also enraged that what was done to me was not, in the eyes of Irish law, 'enough' to amount to rape. I remember reading the statutory definition for rape in college, but it did not register with me then how stupidly narrow that provision is drafted. In France (my native country), rape is any non-consensual 'act of sexual penetration, whatever its nature'. That seems straightforward enough – why the hell would you complicate that? In Ireland, however, in order for the offence to be rape, the penetration must be: '... *by the penis or (...) any object held or manipulated by another person*'.

In other words, if Beast had used a cotton bud that night instead of his fingers, he would be a rapist, but because he opted for the latter, he was not. To be perfectly frank with you, if I had been allowed to weigh in on this odd scenario, I would have much preferred the small and hygienic cotton bud over his dirty fingers and sharp fingernail. Not to mention that with the cotton bud I would have been spared the extra trauma of feeling skin-on-skin contact, the month of PrEP and its side-effects, or the five months of dealing with Doctor Grouch and Clueless Nurse in the clinic of hell, waiting to find out if I had HIV.

And while we're at it, during the lead-up to my trial, the highest court of justice in France, the *Cour de Cassation*, handed down an incomprehensible judgment in October 2020 that the rape of a thirteen-year-old girl by her step-father's tongue did *not* amount to rape because, and I quote, the forcing of his tongue was not 'deemed sufficiently deep to amount to penetration'.[8] This is despite the provision mentioned above clearly reading '*any*' penetration of '*whatever nature*'. There was no sub-section on pulling out the measuring tape. We can safely all guess the gender of the judges on the panel deciding that abomination.

The greatest wrath of all, however, came much later, in the lead-up to the trial during the winter of 2020. I never knew fury like that could exist. At that point, many friends save a loyal handful stopped reaching out altogether. The prospect of a rape trial and my PTSD was just too much for them to handle. But unlike them, I did not have the privilege of being able to forget or disengage from this. And now I had to do it without their support. The heartbreak was such that I walked around with a constant

---

8 *Cour de cassation, Chambre criminelle*, 14 octobre 2020, 20-83.273, Inédit.

lump the size of a basketball in the back of my throat, so painful that it was hard to speak at times. I remember blinking back tears of rage on a daily basis and would regularly explode in the evenings. Like a broken record, I repeated empty questions through angry sobs as my family just listened in sorrowful silence.

'Where ARE they?! Why is no one checking in on me to see how I'm doing?'

I also had no idea how much crap from society rape and sexual violence survivors have to deal with, and at such a vulnerable time when they are trying to pick up the pieces after the most traumatic event of their life.

Trying to prepare myself for the trial, it enraged me to think back on the recent rape trials in Ireland that had savaged survivors' last shred of strength and dignity. The Cork rape trial, where a teenager's underwear was used to argue that wearing a thong implied some form of consent. The Kerry rape trial, where fifty people, including a priest, lined up to shake hands with a convicted sex offender in front of his victim. Lindsay Armstrong, who took her own life at the age of sixteen after the humiliation of being forced to hold up her own underwear in court and repeatedly read the phrase 'little Devil' that was displayed on them. I was livid at the primitive, beastly court system and every single person in it that allowed this barbarity to happen. *J'accuse.*

I'm still angry writing this, evidently. I hate that stereotype of the angry, male-bashing feminist. I love men. I'm a lover of Chimamanda Ngozi Adichie and her graceful poise in defending women's rights, but the fury over the injustices I was faced with consumed my soul for a time. This chapter was, by a mile, the hardest one to write. I am pouring myself raw into this book in the hope that it opens up a dialogue, or at least helps someone else going through this. I'm giving it everything I have, but in the process of doing so it meant reopening closed wounds and digging deep into them. I have pulled things out of those wounds that I didn't even realise were buried in there. Even today. Things I had pushed deep down in order to survive. But this isn't about survival anymore. It's about healing and moving on.

* * *

Anger lives in the body. Not in your airy-fairy, metaphorical sense. It *physically* resides in your body. It is visceral, gripping your insides like vengeful fire and, if not managed, it can lead to pain and even sickness over time. Long-term anger has been scientifically shown to affect cardiac health and increase the risk of heart attack – it literally hurts your heart. It can also increase your blood pressure, weaken your immune system and raise your risk of stroke. A group of Harvard University scientists found that anger can even damage lung functioning and cause asthma, due to chronic airways obstruction and an adverse impact on the inflammatory processes.[9]

There is nothing wrong with being angry in the moment, but we do need to put in place the right outlets to deal with it safely. Anger often hides something. It usually acts as a way-marker, it is trying to communicate with us that there is some primary emotion that we have not processed, like extreme sadness or pain.

There is the concept in yoga called *flow*. A similar concept of flow is also found in positive psychology, which is the mental state reached when you are totally immersed in whatever activity you are doing. Similar to mindfulness, flow requires your mind and body to work as one in complete

---

9 *Angry breathing: a prospective study of hostility and lung function in the Normative Aging Study* (BMJ Publishing Group and British Thoracic Society, 2006).

concentration. We have all experienced that lovely, lucid sensation of being 'in the zone', where we forget ourselves and time seems to fly.

In yoga, flow applies to all things – the breath, time, nature, your thoughts, movement and emotions, including anger. Emotions are never static, they flow. If you repress them or ignore them, you are blocking that flow. They have nowhere else to go, so they become compressed, simmering beneath the surface like pockets of lava. They must be felt and expressed, or they risk erupting like a pressure cooker. When we allow emotions to flow through us without dodging them or clinging onto them, we feel connected to ourselves and what surrounds us. I like to think of it as surfing – if you allow yourself to feel your balance and keep moving and adjusting accordingly, you're gliding on water, but brace or overthink things and you'll lose that balance and fall.

I was clinging onto my rage because without it, there would have been nothing left but to feel how alone I was. And I wasn't ready to do that. Anger kept me company. It kept me warm at night. Angry people are often hurting. The next time you cross paths with an angry person, be kind to them, because you have no idea what's going on behind closed doors. I said above that anger often hides something, well, in my case it was hiding a broken heart. Not just over what Beast did to me, but over the friends who stayed away, the people who refused to listen, those who tried to make my story about themselves or told me what I couldn't do, who got in my way instead of *helping* me. It was too painful for me to feel that loss and emptiness. Instead, I turned to anger because anger is a great motivator.

Ultimately, this period of rage I entered into was the catalyst for my making. Anger is fire, and it is in that fire that I was forged. It took me plunging into the depths of hell and clawing my way back to achieve my greatest triumph in life – forgiveness.

So, that's all well and good to rationalise emotions so simply, but how do you do that in practice? For me, it was through trial and error (and a spectacular amount of the latter). Over time, I figured out a pattern that worked for me, and that may be useful to you too.

First, and like most things, you will have to acknowledge the emotion. You cannot let go of something if you're not aware it's there, or if you're denying it's there, or if you don't realise that you are holding onto it. That requires a little mindfulness. And you don't have to meditate for hours a day to get there, you can 'check in' on your emotions here and there, briefly but effectively. A great practice to get into is to pause a couple of times a day, maybe close your eyes, and ask yourself, 'How am I feeling right now?'. Do this often and you'll quickly get into a discipline of self-awareness.

Second, and far easier said than done, is to allow yourself to feel that emotion. This is the exact opposite of avoidance, so it's no easy feat. An image often used in yoga is that your awareness is like a stage. Emotions that are bottled up within are calling to you to allow them to express them-selves on that stage. Two things can happen: you can keep pushing the emotion away, in which case it will drag you off-stage with it and you will end up acting out on the emotion without realising it (think shouting, hitting something or storming off); or you can say, 'The stage is yours, off you go. But you must come here, to the centre of my awareness, to express yourself.' As soon as you give the emotion the space and attention it was craving, it immediately loses its intensity. And once it's done expressing itself, it begins to dissipate.

The third step is to find positive outlets for it. Once the emotion has expressed itself, it no longer serves you and you need to let it go. You will have to go both outwards and inwards on this one. Outward outlets, like exercise or breathwork, can help to get the trapped energy and tensions from emotion out of the physical body. Inward outlets, such as therapy, journaling or talking to friends, can allow the emotion to regulate itself internally. It's like exploratory surgery – it is painful, but it allows you to identify the source of your anger, and once you hone in on it, that's when the anger starts to dissipate. You need to ask the who, what and why. Who has made you angry? What are you angry about? Why are you angry? Once you find your anger's source, you will get start to get a handle on it because you have uncovered the information it is trying to relay to you.

A word of warning on this third step – as wonderful as these outlets are, on their own they are not enough. They will only work where you have let the emotion express itself first. In the months leading up to the trial, I found myself exercising compulsively every day. Each time someone told me that I could not do something (could not speak publicly, could not protect my therapy notes, could not say I was a victim of sexual violence), I did sit-ups out of frustration. In the face of feeling so powerless, it gave me the illusion that I still had some form of control. But exercising did not rid my heart of the rage it carried. That only came after the trial ended, when I could stop to breathe and unpack it all through counselling.

Of those three steps, the second is the one I probably struggled with the most. How on Earth do you let yourself feel anger without losing your calm? I had no idea. I had never dealt with rage on this scale before. How can you feel something like this without punching a hole in the wall? I raised this with my therapist one day, which led to one of the most eye-opening experiences I've ever had.

'It's exactly like sadness, you have to sit with it,' she explained.

'I do not understand. How can you *sit* with this? Sadness is low energy. You can feel it calmly, therefore you can sit with it. With anger, I want to sprint a marathon and punch someone at the finish line.'

'Let's do it right now. Close your eyes for me.'

I indulge her, rolling my eyes before I close them.

'OK, now picture something that angered you, but not something too big, like the rape. For example, think about a friend who made you angry recently, on a scale of three out of ten or so.'

Well, I'm spoilt for choice here, so many memories to pick from. I settle on one.

'Got it.'

'OK, now just think about that for a while. Get comfortable and let it sit with you a while.'

'Fine.'

'Observe your body. Talk me through what's happening. What are you feeling?'

'What do you mean?'

'When you turn your attention inwards and listen to your body, are you feeling any internal sensations as you sit with this anger?'

I frowned through closed eyes and listened in a little more carefully. And then I felt it. A warm tingling in the palms of my hands and soles of my feet. I'm a cold creature – my extremities are normally icicles. I've made fully grown men spring out of bed shrieking by rolling over in my sleep and accidentally brushing my foot against their leg.

'My feet and hands feel hot.'

'OK, stay with it. Just observe what's happening.'

The tingling heat started getting hotter. How weird.

'It's getting warmer, it feels like the ground and armrests are heated, but I can tell it's coming from me.'

'You're doing great, keep going.'

I felt it moving.

Holy shit, it's moving! 'I've never felt this before. The heat is starting to move.'

'Where?'

'Upwards.'

'OK, keep going.'

I gulped. I was not comfortable with this at all. The heat was that strong it almost felt like the burn of ice. The tingling was getting so intense, surely the armchair must be vibrating? How high up was this jamboree going to travel exactly?

'It's up to my knees and arms now. The tingling is super strong. It's really weird, I've never experienced this before. I don't know why it's moving.'

'Don't let your "thinking mind" interfere, just allow yourself to feel it and observe without judging what's happening in each moment.'

'I'm scared.'

'It's OK to be afraid, but you are absolutely safe. This is a healthy way of dealing with anger. If it gets too overwhelming for you, we can stop the exercise at any time, but you're doing great.'

We continued. I sat there, incredulous, as the heat moved progressively up into my thighs and elbows, to my hips and upper arms, and then my core and shoulders. At this stage the tingling turned into an internal earthquake.

'It's in my stomach and collarbone now.'

After a few minutes, the two sources of heat joined each other in my neck, connecting into one slow-swirling ball of fire in the back of my throat. I could feel the flush of heat in my cheeks.

'It's not moving anymore. It's just stuck there.'

'That's OK, stay with it.'

I stayed with it for I couldn't tell you how long. Might have been thirty seconds, but it felt like a number of minutes. And then the seismic fireball started to dwindle slightly. Almost imperceptible at first, but after a few seconds it was unmistakably losing power.

'The intensity is going down, slowly. It's starting to move back down, I think.'

The heat moved back down through my shoulders and arms, core and legs, until it reached my hands and feet again.

'We're back to the palms and feet. It's continuing to weaken.'

'Keep going until it's finished.'

Like the embers of a fire dying out, the energy slowly dissipated until it eventually disappeared as it had appeared, back down into the armrests and the ground.

'It's gone.'

'Keep your eyes closed until you're ready to open them. Don't rush it. Just sit with the stillness for a while.'

An overwhelming sense of calm had taken over. My entire body was warm, as though from the glowing cinders left behind the fireball's trajectory. It was similar to the pleasant blanket of shock I was wrapped in after the night of the attack. I stayed there a few more minutes in silence before slowly blinking my eyes open.

'Wow.'

'How do you feel?'

'So … calm.'

She nodded wisely. 'How did you find the exercise?'

'I've never experienced anything like that in my life. The tingling and heat were so strong.'

'That's the manifestation of anger. It has very physical effects on the body. Sometimes we don't notice it because we're trying to avoid it, and it builds up over time. But you can *see* anger – you can see angry people in the street. It's written all over their bodies and faces.'

I was serene for days after that. Have you ever walked out of an ice-cold shower and felt that ecstatic relief as your body is no longer in pain? It took me knowing the rage that burned in the pit of my stomach to no longer get angry over daily things. Now, I want to flag here that although highly effective, this exercise can get extremely overwhelming if tackling anger that is too great. I am a certified yoga teacher, and despite only dealing with an incident that registered as a magnitude of three out of ten on the Sarah scale of fury, I found it quite scary. For things like the assault, the nines and tens out of ten, this exercise should only be undertaken with a professional at first. However, you can use this technique on the smaller angers and empty the rage tank a little. It's a fantastic way to clear some salt so that the ash can do its thing.

* * *

It's been over two years since the assault but to this day, anger is still something I struggle with sometimes. Some days I feel resentment towards all the 'salt-bearers', as I called them – those toxic people and friends who hurt me or let me down. But in the end, this isn't about them, this is about me. In the end, the focus for me became not being altered by this. I refused to let this or Beast or the salt-bearers or the fire change who I am. I had a choice to make, and you have one too. You can let them break you and turn you into the next pillar of salt, or you can choose to let go, to forgive and to flourish from this.

Forgiveness is one of the hardest things you will ever have to do, but it can be done. In many ways, I found it easier to forgive Beast, who, until the trial, I pictured as some dumbass, limited creature incapable of real malice or calculation. Much harder to forgive were the educated, privileged people and institutions who were supposed to protect me but failed to do so – friends, legal professionals, people I looked up to, the criminal courts and criminal justice staff.

There will be days where you choke on angry tears because it isn't fair. Walking through fire like this is transformational, it can make you grow exponentially, if you find the strength to let go. I choose to forgive, to let go, so that I am not weighed down. I choose to practice compassion so that I can uplift myself. I make that choice daily. Some days it comes easy, other days it's a Herculean task.

You do not have to let this define you. Not this, not your fear, not your sadness, not your anger, not your grief. In the immediate aftermath of an assault, you may feel like all you can do is cling onto any raft for dear life, but with the passing of time you will come to realise that you are so much more than your trauma.

Something I repeat often in my yoga classes is: You are not your thoughts and you are not your emotions. You are the space that holds them all, and then some. You are your hopes, your dreams and your memories. You are light and darkness, ash and salt, fire and phoenix. You are holy. You are stardust that has moved through cosmic clouds and supernovas, literally. This mind and body of yours are sacred ground. They were crafted by the gods, and you will not let them fall to some ignorant, unawakened table salt. You are an extremely complex being, full of beautiful contradictions. You are movement, the perpetual flow of energy, constantly changing and shifting. You are never-ending strength and courage to show up for yourself on days when no one else will.

I am Sarah Grace. I am fierce. I am a lawyer, yoga teacher and now published author. I am survivor, daughter, sister, friend, forgiver, empowerer of women and warrior. I am the million moments of joy throughout my day, the calm in the face of adversity, the feisty sassiness that makes my friends laugh, the strength to choose forgiveness over anger.

SURVIVAL GUIDE: ANGER

I am focusing on anger here, but this piece works for many of the 'negative' emotional states, like depression, anxiety or grief. There is no magical cure-all for these extreme emotional states. It takes time to work through them and a lot of self-compassion, support and therapy. Below are some of the things that helped me work through my anger, and so maybe they can help you too.

Acknowledge it: the first thing about anger, just like depression, grief or anxiety, is to recognise it. Sometimes these emotions sneak up on us and we don't even realise they're there. Try pausing for a couple of minutes and asking yourself how you are feeling. Just observe how you are, do not judge how you are feeling. Remind yourself there's nothing wrong with your feelings, you are entitled to feel this way. Observe the emotion(s) that arises when you do this.

Say the words: a proven strategy to deal with difficult emotions is to put words on them, whether you write them down or communicate them to a friend or therapist. This is empowering not only by helping you to define the boundaries around what you are (and are not) feeling, but also by reminding you that you are not alone in feeling this way.

Try mindfulness: whatever it is you are feeling, it is valid and under-standable. There is a lot to be angry about. Emotions need to be felt before we can let them go, or they will just come back harder. Try a mindfulness class, or just allow yourself to sit with the emotion and feel

it, even if only for a few minutes to start with. There is also an abun-
dance of wonderful guided meditation and mindfulness on apps like
Headspace, Calm or Peptalk.

Write it down: you may feel as though you are making no progress, but
you are. Healing is not linear and you will need real evidence of your
progress to hold on to when dealing with a monster like rage, grief or
depression. It will also be useful if there is to be a trial. What makes
you angry now could help you do something useful in future.

Breathe: I know, it sounds so easy and condescending, right? *'Just breathe.'*
But there's a reason people keep saying it. Your breath regulates your
nervous system, and you can tap into it at any time. Start small and try
taking three slow, deep breaths here and there. Try lengthening your
exhale to double the length of the inhale by breathing in through the
nose and out slowly through the mouth. If you experience a burst of
anger, try centring yourself and calming the body by closing your eyes
and try taking 10 'belly breaths': on each inhale, breathe down deeply
into the lower belly rather than the chest. More breathing techniques
are given in the Survival Guide for Chapter 4.

Get physical: it doesn't necessarily have to be exercise. But anger is
energy and it needs an outlet to be channelled through. Once you have
acknowledged the emotion and allowed yourself to feel it, deep clean
the house, try that kick-boxing class, go for a brisk walk, cook something that involves some serious elbow grease like whisking, the point
is to *move*.

Get counselling: however mentally resilient you are, no one is superhuman. If you want to explore therapy, there are some excellent organisations, like the Rape Crisis Centres, which helped me, that specialise in sexual trauma and offer counselling tailored for the anger, grief or anxiety you are feeling. (See the Survival Guide at the end of Chapter 4 for how to ensure that your therapy notes are not made available to the Defence in the event of a trial.)

Communicate: emotions on this scale are difficult to convey to someone who has not experienced them because it's almost impossible to relate to something like this. Short of giving them this book (and pointing them to Chapter 6, which speaks specifically to the role of family and friends), what's important to get across is that trauma does not go away in a few months. Flag from the outset that this is new territory for you too, and that you need your loved ones to be patient and supportive. They may need some reminders as time goes on.

6.

Dear All: Advice for the Survivor's Support Network

Diary entry, 10 October 2019:
'Where is everyone?'

I'm back in the office one week after the attack. In hindsight – absolutely crackers. I lost count of the panic attacks, the exhaustion and nausea from the PrEP medication, the flashbacks that terrorised my days and the nightmares that haunted my nights. But I could not bear the idea of being alone with my thoughts. After days of begging me to stay off work a little longer, my parents, who still don't know about the violation, eventually concede and drop me back to the apartment before travelling back to France. I want to reclaim it. I don't want to let Beast win. I love that place – we scoured the dismal Dublin rental market for ages to find it, I'll be damned if we let him scare us off it now.

Those next few weeks, the angel that is Niamh sleeps next to me at night, so I somewhat manage the fear of that room, but during the day any sound from the street sends me into a frenzy. I compulsively check that the windows and doors are locked, sometimes twenty to thirty times a day. I need to be in an office, surrounded by people, albeit behind glass walls at a safe colleague-distance. Terrified of being betrayed by the bruises on my neck, I decide to wear silk scarves for the first week back in work. I'll continue to wear them long after the bruises have faded away. In mid-August. Even for Ireland, it's too hot. I convince myself that I can pull them off as a fashion statement but, looking in the mirror, no matter how I rearrange them, I look like an air-hostess.

In the office, people are afraid of me. It's brutal. Women, in particular, cannot meet my gaze, which does not help my growing sense of shame. I remember one senior colleague saw me walking down the corridor, locked eyes with me, visibly panicked, turned on her heel and practically ran in the opposite direction. Talk about making someone feel like an untouchable.

By not mentioing the sexual assault, I feel like I'm lying by omission, to everyone. I don't want to lie, but I don't want to be branded a rape victim either. I'm not ready for the truth to come out. I don't know if I can live it down. I give everyone the same 'vanilla' version of events that I gave my parents. To cover the sexual assault piece, I settle on 'the unspeakable didn't happen'. Dignified. Poetic, even. Also, not a lie. As we've seen, in Ireland, what happened to me is not 'legally' rape.

Mercifully, a brave handful of colleagues make a beeline for me or drop by my office to offer support. I could kiss them if it wasn't for my aversion to touching. I can just about shake hands now, but any contact beyond the wrist makes my skin crawl.

Those next few months are like walking the tightrope between knowing

I can kick a rapist's ass and yet feeling incredibly vulnerable. I often need to stand with my back to the wall in meetings and in crowded rooms (incidentally, quite the power move). The stress from covering up the truth and the worry that I would never recover translated into very physical symptoms – chest pains, stomach pains, nausea, headaches and dizziness, like I was about to faint. You name it, I probably had it.

It had never occurred to me until then that survivors don't just have to cope with their own trauma, they also have to shoulder the burden of other people's reaction to what happened to them. The reactions I received were as unpredictable as they were wide-ranging – some were helpful, some well-intentioned, some anti-climactic, some hurtful, and some made me so angry it was hard to breathe.

* * *

I've talked a lot so far about the experience of rape and sexual assault from a survivor's perspective. I hope it illustrates a little more to someone who has not had to walk through that kind of fire what a survivor goes through, and that it is much more complex and layered than the stereotype it's often made out to be.

Now, I want to flip the perspective and speak to the friends, families, partners and colleagues of survivors. Your role is central to the survivor's recovery. We, the survivors, have been banished to the Shadowland, and each of you holds the lever to the drawbridge that we can cross back into the world of the living. You may feel powerless in the face of what has happened, but in reality you are the safe harbour from which a thousand rescue ships are launched.

Rape and sexual violence destroy a person's identity. It strips them of their human dignity because someone has essentially used them as an object, and it cuts them off from their emotions through dissociation. It destroys their place in the world by uprooting their grounding and collapsing their landmarks, starting with their very own mind and body, and so it is a form of death. After the attack, I was no longer Sarah. I was a sexual violence victim, just trying to figure out where she stood.

This is where you, the supporters, come in. The good news is that there is much you can do to create a safe space for the survivor, in which they can focus all their attention on experimenting with their new boundaries and, in time, learning how to transcend them. I know for a fact that I would not have felt a lot of the rage I explored in the previous chapter had I not been let down so spectacularly by some of my close ones, and the only thing that helped dim those flames of fury was the support I received from some pretty amazing people.

So, I want to walk you through some examples of behaviours that I encountered in my journey, the good, the bad and the neutral, to show what works and what doesn't for the survivor's recovery in various scenarios. This is a topic that came up frequently in discussions with friends and family and threaded through this chapter are some of their own perspectives and experiences.

SPEAK UP, REACH OUT

The first issue I want to address is, personally speaking, probably the one that comes up the most – not knowing what to do. Many in my circle spoke of this, that they had no idea how to behave or how to approach the subject with me, that is if they should even mention it at all.

It is totally understandable not to know how to handle something like this. We were taught a lot of questionably useful knowledge in school – trigonometry, the mitochondria being the powerhouse of the cell – but never how to act with someone who has just experienced life-changing trauma. When you think about how many people have such experiences, be it rape or a death in the family or what have you, you wonder why learning to play the tin whistle took priority over that. Fortunately, things are starting to change, but only because people like you and me are willing to have a conversation about it.

Speaking about any trauma is hard, especially sexual trauma. Unless you have been through it yourself, it will be near-impossible to fully relate. However, from the survivor's perspective, the best thing you can do is to fight your instincts to be distant or give them space. Trauma like this is already the most isolating thing for survivors because it is invisible. The loss is not tangible – there are no external markings, no one has passed away. And yet, you feel as though you have died, and it is the loneliest thing in the world for that not to be acknowledged.

When I returned to work, while some mentors and colleagues were stellar, many kept their distance or avoided me altogether. People knew I had been assaulted in my bed and that *something* had happened, but not how far the assault went. Some avoided eye contact or danced around the subject, others froze or scuttled away when it came up. Their avoidance was a death sentence – I was condemned to the shadows of inexistence by their refusal to acknowledge that my life, as I knew it, had ended. Worse still, shortly after the assault, once the initial shock of my story had passed, some friends completely disappeared. I had shielded my family from the awful truth, I lived in a different country than my parents and sister, so I depended on friends' emotional support to get through this. It was in that period that I needed them most, and yet I have never felt so alone than in those months. 'Where is everyone?' I would find myself murmuring repeatedly in disbelief. I know, now, that the vast majority of those reactions came from a place of fear. Many were uncomfortable, unsure how to proceed, or even afraid to confront the fact that this could happen to them. Other reactions came from noble intentions, like not wanting to overwhelm or embarrass *me*. But at the time, to me, it all felt like abandonment and betrayal.

I don't blame anyone for being afraid. Rape is still a taboo subject for a reason, we all recoil at the word because for many of us it is one of our worst fears. But the problem with withdrawal and avoiding the subject is that it will only ever trigger more secrecy, more shame and more anger in the survivor. It forces women and victims to stay silent, which is just another form of abuse, even if unintentional. Like you, it can be hard for us to say the words. Sometimes we haven't even admitted it to ourselves because we are so terrified of being judged, rejected, not believed or even blamed. We don't want to trigger or shock you, or to make you feel uncomfortable. So we conceal our ugly secret behind a thick veil of apparent functionality or misperceived aloofness, and erase a part of ourselves in the process. It is one of the reasons why so alarmingly few victims report having been sexually assaulted, only 49% of women and 19% of men.[10]

When you do reach out to a survivor, however, you are bridging that chasm between them and society. Just as your silence risks pushing us deeper into exile, your choice to say something is our salvation. By forsak-

---

10 According to a study conducted by Trinity College Dublin and NUI Maynooth in 2020.

ing your comfort zone and acknowledging the sexual assault, calmly and with compassion, you have lowered the drawbridge and signalled that it's OK for us to speak about it. Your allyship and courage in normalising the conversation makes us feel safe with you, and in turn we want to follow your example.

Instead of suggesting words to start that conversation, I'll quote directly from a friend who, when sitting across from me at lunch one day, leaned in and said, 'I hope you don't mind me saying this, I heard you were assaulted and I just want to say I hope you're doing OK.' Mind? I could have bear-hugged him. Another friend confidently strolled into my office the day I came back to work and openly asked me questions about what had happened, without flinching or tiptoeing around the subject. His comfort in my presence and keeping eye-contact relieved a lot of my unease.

For those of you who are worried about saying the wrong thing – let me reassure you that the only wrong thing you can say is nothing. Words are important, yes, but what truly matters is the intention behind them. At such a vulnerable time in our life, all we seek from you is warmth and comfort and presence. We are not looking to you to find a solution, because there is none. You do not need to fashion a beautifully crafted speech. The words you say will be the right ones because *you* chose them. Whatever they are, what they will really say is: 'I am not afraid. I am choosing to stand with you. You are safe with me and I embrace you for who you are.'

I described earlier the senior colleague who saw me in the corridor and hurried away without saying a word. If she had swung by my office once she had recomposed herself to say something, *anything*, even days later, it would have appeased some of my own deep-cutting shame. She probably thought about it, but in the end didn't do it because the fear of being embarrassed or uncomfortable was just too strong. Perhaps she wished someone had reassured *her* on what to do, just as I needed her to reassure me that I still had a future ahead. In contrast, another manager, who is also a friend and mentor, calmly listened as I opened up about my story and paused before saying, 'I think you're just remarkable'. The people who did make me feel accepted, the colleagues who went out of their way in a personal capacity to speak up, thank you, for your words that have carried me to where I am today.

Words, speech, are liberating. I attended a suicide prevention training workshop a while back and one sentence resonated with me: the word 'suicide' is never going to put suicidal thoughts in someone's head. That person either is feeling suicidal, in which case the thought is already in their mind, or they are not. If they are, saying the word rather than dancing around the subject will be a relief because it will take the intensity out of it. It's very similar with 'rape' and 'sexual assault'. Saying the words (considerately) is not going to trigger a survivor. If you are worried that you are using a wrong term, do not be afraid to ask the survivor. That small gesture is hugely inclusive and shows you're thinking of them. Personally, I really hated the word 'assault', for example, because it can mean anything from groping to digital rape. But that's a purely personal thing. No one can reproach you for speaking from the heart.

If you are still struggling to find the words, allow me to offer a few pointers that were said to me to start you off:

I love you.

I care about you.

This changes nothing as to the incredible person you are, and you will only come out of this stronger.

You are so brave. I think your courage is inspirational.

I'm not great with words, but I want you to know I am here for you.

I am full of admiration for you.

You are not alone.

You are safe with me.

I am so sorry he did that to you.

I hope you know how loved you are.

What you're going through is awful, but it won't last forever, and I have every faith in you that you can do this.

You are an amazing person and you are not defined by this.

I know you have the strength to overcome this, even if you don't see it right now.

Take your pick and repeat as often as necessary. Send the text. Pick up the phone. Sit next to them and be present. Make eye contact. Show them you are comfortable with them. Just *say* something. You have no idea how much that can mean to someone recovering from trauma.

DEALING WITH OUTBURSTS

The next thing I want to unravel is how all-encompassing sexual trauma is. It's difficult to explain how deep it runs. Overnight, my entire world became defined by reference to the attack. If my existence was a Cartesian system, that single point in time was my 0:0:0 coordinate point, the place from which everything originated and everything was measured against.

I was so frozen in that oblivion that I saw everything through the lens of the assault. Small gestures of kindness, like someone dropping a coffee at my desk, just because, had me teary-eyed with gratitude that they had remembered I was going through a rough time. Equally, every time someone behaved discourteously, stole credit for an idea I had or took advantage of my generosity, I resented it bitterly. From where I stood, I was just trying to keep my head above water after a traumatising violation and near-death experience. I could not understand why someone who had the luxury of not enduring that ordeal couldn't put themselves in my shoes for five minutes and just not be a dick.

I forgot that *they* had forgotten that everything in my life revolved around the attack. I thought it was obvious from the deep trenches carved into my face and the light gone from my eyes. People forget, and that's normal. But the assault is *always* there for the survivor. We have no escape from it, no respite. Every waking moment, the repercussions of it are on our minds. As a result, we may have sudden reactions or outbursts that seem to come completely out of the blue. Sometimes they come as a surprise even to the survivor.

Initially, these outbursts may seem irrational, but on closer inspection they make complete sense. A paramedic once said to me that after a rape or traumatic sexual assault, you become a ticking time-bomb. It's possible that you'll never blow up but, equally, the smallest trigger could detonate you at any moment. When these explosions occur, be it in the form of panic attacks, waves of depression, bursting into tears or lashing out, the survivor has lost the handle on their trauma. It bucks and thrashes under them like a wild horse, and both the survivor and their loved ones can get hurt in this ferocious rodeo.

I found that things I would once have dealt with calmly were now the match that would set me ablaze. The sound of a woman screaming in a movie scene brought me back to my screams on that fateful night. Micro-aggressions in my day-to-day reminded me how little people cared about what I was going through. The commotion of a crowded nightclub had me panicked that someone would touch my neck. Overhearing crude locker-room talk or men using the word 'bitch' reminded me of the daily, incessant battle women have to fight against casual misogyny, sexual violence and objectification.

These triggers had not just a mental but also a physical toll. I often failed to realise that as I bottled up my emotions, so as not to cause a scene, I was also holding my breath or clenching my jaw. I did not notice that when I talked about the assault, I would hyperventilate and become breathless and dizzy. To this day I still do that sometimes. The body carries the perpetual weight of these emotions and trauma, and eventually it takes its revenge by blowing up. Back to our volcanic eruption in Chapter 5 – they are the residual pockets of lava rumbling underneath the ash. They lurk under the surface, unnoticed by the outside world, and make us disproportionately hypersensitive to everything, including things seemingly unrelated to the assault.

I had a violent panic attack while watching *Parasite* with friends a good seven months after the assault. There is no rape scene in that movie, and yet the premise of a house being infiltrated unknown to the people living in it had me in fits of panic in the cinema. That was the first time I saw it register in my friends' eyes how much vulnerability and pain I was in every day. It stayed with them a while, I'm sure, but slowly they moved on, back to the land of the living. I was not able to follow. I was stuck in the Shadowland, haunted by that scene for months afterwards.

On that note, I often get asked how to support a survivor who gets triggered. While this is hugely personal, as a general rule of thumb try to avoid saying 'Calm down' or 'Just breathe'. I have yet to meet one person who actually likes that. Instead, what you can do is be their anchor to reality by standing near them and staying very calm. You can influence their breathing wordlessly, just by slowing down your own breathing. If you do speak, stick to short, positive statements, such as 'I'm right here' or 'I've got you'. Most people don't want to be touched during a panic attack. Let yourself be guided by the person. Your best bet is to ask what works for them, but not until after the storm has passed. When it has, remind them you are neither embarrassed or scared, that you're very comfortable to just be with them, or hold their hand, whatever they need. (See also the Survival Guide for Chapter 4, which sets out breathing tips for panic attacks.)

More generally, you can support the survivor by just being a little extra gentle and considerate in your interactions with them. You don't have to lay it on thick, but a little kindness often goes a long way. Give them praise where it's due if they do well, thank them properly if they help you out with something, be warm and friendly when speaking with them. Be alert to their body language. When I tensed up in social gatherings, I was so grateful when people noticed and asked how I was feeling. I felt safe with them because I knew I had someone in the room watching out for me.

You can also be mindful of triggers or circumstances specific to the survivor's case. I could give so many examples here. The two friends who, when arranging my accommodation at their wedding, made sure that I wasn't in a ground-floor room or near the noisy reception, and had trusted friends in the adjacent rooms. The wonderful friend who saw me getting overwhelmed about writing this book one evening and just pulled me into his arms, letting me sob into his chest for a good fifteen minutes as he stroked my hair. The friends who invited me to their family homes on the bank holidays, because they knew my parents lived overseas and didn't want me to be alone in my apartment. Those who kept a note in their calendar of the anniversary of the attack and sent a thoughtful text on the day. All those moments are seared into my mind as the lifebuoys that were thrown to me in the shipwreck.

You are even the supporters of survivors you have never met, every time you speak up against sexism or victim-blaming, which is the breeding ground for sexual violence culture. There are so many voices spewing outrageous absurdities on a daily basis, from the media to social media, and people we know, too. It is important that we all speak out against those 'small' moments that feed into the wider culture. I remember friends would jump in to interrupt conversations when they heard sexist comments they knew would press my buttons. Even more important to me are the men brave enough to stand with women by calling out comments that cross the line or by encouraging a conversation about the experience of women with their other male friends. We need your voice to drown the toxic ones out and amplify survivors'.

DON'T LET GO

Next on my list is what to do when the survivor withdraws from friends and family. This is classic in people with PTSD or dissociation. To put it in context, sexual trauma is often uncharted waters for the survivor. They have no idea how to cope. In the process of figuring it out, they can feel they are a strain on loved ones, feel ashamed or struggle to connect to their old life. So they withdraw from family and friends, or stop engaging in activities they used to enjoy.

In the periods when I withdrew, I did so because I believed no one could understand what I was going through. Friends can't relate. Family can't relate. It's too damn big. There was no point in kidding myself that I wasn't completely alone, or that people wouldn't eventually get tired of my inability to move past my trauma, so as a defence mechanism I pulled away first. No one can drop me if I beat them to it, right? Genius logic, I know. But in truth, all I wanted, all anyone wants really, was for someone to listen to the unspoken sorrows of my soul. I was dying for someone to hold me in their arms, to have a connection with another human again, it really was that simple. I was craving for people to see me, all of me, the ash and the salt and the blooming shoots, so that maybe through their eyes I could see myself again too.

As a survivor's support network, this is one of the areas where you can have the most impact. Face-to-face support is one of the most crucial aspects of healing from PTSD, so your role, if you choose it, is to bring that person back into the fold. There are a few ways to do this. The first is to be aware of the general signs of withdrawal. Keep an eye out for periods when the survivor starts to fall off the grid. You might be at a social event, for example, and notice that their eyes have glazed over. They may appear lost in thought, but really they are lost in the weeds of their trauma. They might stop responding to texts, particularly in group chats. They may avoid social gatherings altogether and put a remarkable amount of effort into distancing themselves from certain people. This can often be accompanied by a cover-up of 'I'm really busy right now' or 'I'm fine'.

Now, you obviously want to strike a balance here. Clearly, you want to respect the person's boundaries. But equally, you can't leave it on the survivor to suffer through this alone. The natural human reaction will be to give them space because *you* don't want to overburden them, but often that is the very reason they distanced themselves in the first place. That vicious circle needs to be nipped in the bud.

You really cannot go wrong with reaching out and being inclusive. Ideally, offer an out so they don't feel pressured. For example, send texts rather than call. If they don't want to engage, they won't read your message, but at least they know you're thinking of them. That's a real reminder they are not alone. Personally, when people gently pointed out that I was withdrawing and asked if I was OK, or offered that we step outside together, it went straight to my heart because someone had noticed my absence and, not only that, *wanted* to pull me back in.

Some magical friends of mine also understood that 'is there anything I can do?', although well-intentioned, put the onus back on me to ask for help. Instead, they were proactive and took it on themselves to reach out, allowing me to lean on someone other than myself for a change. They made suggestions that put the decision-making power firmly back in my court, like 'I'm coming over unless you tell me not to', or 'I'll call you at 8.00pm tonight', or 'We're going for a walk and you can talk about it if you want to', or 'I'll tell this manager you had bad news and need to step out for a breather'. Prior to social events, they suggested we walk there together or met up beforehand. They regularly kept me on the grid with texts like, 'You don't need to respond, I just want you to know I'm thinking of you'. The point is, you can respect someone's space but still be supportive.

My other advice is to try not to get defensive if or when the person withdraws. Despite repeatedly fighting against my feeling detached from everything, I lost many of those battles with myself. I found it impossible to connect with anything unrelated to my grappling with having nearly been killed. Promotions in work became meaningless, friends' obsessions with buying houses and having babies were utterly superficial, the dating scene was an absurd repetition in terrible decisions, and projects in my personal life that had previously excited me turned to ash in my mouth. That offended some people. They saw my disconnect as disdain for their life goals or trivialising their life choices and, in fairness to them, that's probably close to what it was at the time.

But what they failed to understand is that dissociation isn't real. It is a disruption of the brain function in response to trauma, and it's something survivors have very little control over. You have to remember that this volatile behaviour is not personal. It is not targeted at you. It has absolutely nothing to do with you. It is simply highlighting how alone and out of place the survivor feels.

I'm not saying this means you shut down your own feelings. Of course, everyone has their own stuff going on, but the worst thing you can do is disengage or let go at a time when that person needs you most. To give another example, one of the most crushing responses I received was when asking a friend for comfort during a fit of tears one evening and she replied, 'I can't be there for you right now, I'm going through my own stuff.' I don't doubt that was true, but a far softer (let alone more effective) way to communicate that would have been to say instead: 'I really want to be there for you, but I'm not feeling very strong right now. Can I help you with a smaller aspect or a particular thing you're struggling with?' You don't have to take on all of the survivor's troubles, but you can still meet each other halfway and act as supports for each other.

CHECK YOUR EXPECTATIONS AT THE DOOR

The bottom line is, you simply cannot know what a survivor is going through. Each experience is unique and deeply personal. You must check your assumptions at the door and assume that you know nothing. Even if you have dealt with a sexual violence or assault survivor before, trauma affects us all differently and you must let yourself be guided by the survivor on this one. A lot of people who went MIA after the attack explained their behaviour with statements like, 'If it was me, I wouldn't want people to contact me.' But they *hadn't* been through something like this. And even if they had, what they might want doesn't mean it's what I would want too.

Similarly, when I told people what had happened in the months that followed the attack, the instinctive reaction for many was to ask me if I had moved out of my apartment yet. They were adamant that I had to do this immediately, but the truth was that I didn't want to move out. This was *my* place, dammit, I wasn't about to let some Beast spook me out of it. It might have seemed counterintuitive to them, but that was key to my healing – to take a stand and fight my dissociation by rekindling some bonds with the place. Another survivor may have felt very differently. You need to trust that the survivor knows what is best for them.

You will also have to accept that the survivor may say or do things that might upset you. My family opened my eyes on this one. I didn't tell them about the violation for a year. One, because they lived abroad and as a mild control-freak I didn't want to tell them without being there to monitor how they were coping afterwards. But two, and far more importantly, I did not want to land a bomb like that on their laps and risk flooding their land-scape with ashes, too. One person down in the family was enough. They didn't see it that way. As amazing as they were when I finally coughed up the whole story, Alison did tell me later that she was almost hurt that I had told others before her and our parents. She explained it took her a while to see that I did it not because I wanted to hide the truth from them, but because I was waiting until I was ready, to protect the family.

Survivors will do things that seem illogical. They might tell different people different things, or at different times. They might pretend to be fine for a long time. Their fundamental views on life or usual behaviours may change drastically. They might hold things back from you, for a great number of reasons. It's important to remember that whatever the reaction is, it does not reflect badly on you. Eruptions are unpredictable, and we are just doing everything we can to cling onto something as the thrashing monster within tries to unseat us.

This is why I would also argue that supporters should consider going for counselling as well. Exactly like the survivor, you are going through a period of heavy turmoil. Supporting someone through that darkness has an enormous impact on you and your life, so you need to make sure you have supports in place for yourself.

One person, in particular, awakened me to that. I was often told, 'You're so strong, I forget you've been through this trauma. You carry it like it's nothing to you.' Well, there's one woman who carried it along with me, and that's my sister. She carried not only me but herself as well through the horror of it all. Strength like that does not come often, but there are consequences to it. She was so strong that I almost forgot she came out of it incredibly burnt, too, despite never showing it to me. My family were all warriors, but Alison was a hero.

RELATIONSHIPS AND INTIMATE PARTNERS

As a society, we have a very specific way of depicting sexual violence survivors. It seems victims can only ever be portrayed as the one-dimensional, broken shell of a woman. If I see one more article on sexual assault with a photo of a woman huddled in the foetal position and a tear rolling down her bruised cheek, I swear to Lucifer I'll lose it. I hope that by now I've made it clear that nothing could be more oversimplistic a stereotype than that. The people publishing such images do not realise the harm they are doing. They are feeding that stifling stigma and pushing victims deeper into seclusion, rather than helping us dismantle it by genuinely amplifying survivors' voices.

For a good while, societal expectations made me think I had to behave a certain way. I couldn't reconcile that image of a rape victim with me, so my choices were to either cover it up or to act demure and reserved. I felt shame over what had been done to my body, but the greater guilt came when I started dating again, because it somehow meant that I wasn't 'traumatised enough' or a 'proper' sexual violence victim. When really, survivors should feel free to jump into bed with whoever they want, whenever they want, without judgement from the outside world. If it helps your recovery, you go for it, my love. Chase what brings you healing to the ends of the Earth.

Survivors come from all walks of life, and they are all forces to be reckoned with – CEOs, working moms and dads, extravert business owners and reserved academics, passionate athletes and badass artists, teachers, politicians, students, your neighbour, Lady Gaga. We are not fragile or damaged, we don't need pity, we shouldn't have to put on a brave face or sweep the whole thing under the carpet. We are human, and we need human connections, interactions and contact. It is unrealistic to expect survivors to close ourselves off from relationships just because we were sexually assaulted or raped. As with everything else, you have no idea what goes through another person's mind, so just let yourself be guided by them and keep an open mind.

That perspective was cemented for me by the Dublin Rape Crisis Centre (DRCC). Through my yoga business, the Busy Warrior Yoga, I had run a fundraiser for the DRCC on International Women's Day, eight months after the assault. Afterwards, I swung by their offices to drop off the collection buckets. In the lobby, I bumped into a senior staff member, and after chatting a while she uttered the most transformational words I have heard on my journey.

'I hope you're still getting up to mischief,' she said with a twinkle in her eye. 'I hope you're getting out there and dancing your little heart out and driving all the boys wild.'

MISCHIEF.

What a wonderful word. It had not made an appearance in my vocabulary in a very long time, and yet here was a woman who sees rape victims day in and day out, and she was encouraging me to live my life and stay playful. What an amazing, kickass queen. *That* is the attitude we should be adopting with survivors, not expecting them to stay traumatised forever by their ordeal.

As a sexual assault survivor, romantic relationships are probably the most complex area of healing, and you need to honour yourself on this one. We all naturally desire intimacy, but there is no right or wrong pace to returning to your romantic or sexual life. There is only your own pace. The sole goal is to enjoy yourself, at whatever level you feel ready for. It must feel

200% right, and you must be extraordinarily selfish in communicating what you want and need. Anything less than that, or anyone who tries to tell you any differently, you tell them and the horse they rode in on to take a hike.

As partners, be it short flings or long-term relationships, it's understandable that the impact of your partner's trauma will be on your mind. I'm here to tell you that you do not have to feel daunted or afraid. The survivor is honouring you by letting you walk a part of their healing journey with them, and you can both experience a lot of sexual intimacy, pleasure and fulfilment, particularly if you lay the foundations of safe sex by communicating with each other.

I really surprised myself with this one. I found my sensuality again much faster than I thought I would. Pre-attack, I would have considered myself a fun, flirty, fiercely loyal and passionate person. My romantic life was always hugely important to me and I was terrified that I had lost this big part of myself after the assault. I mean, was it 'normal' or 'OK' for someone who had been violently violated and nearly murdered to want to have a love life again? The answer is yes. It might take you two days, it might take you two years, but whatever version of yourself you want to come back to, you will in time, because that is who you are.

The only thing that is crucial is that whatever you do must be with a person you feel safe with and trust unconditionally. I was lucky in that department because I had someone with whom I shared a special connection, and I knew in my gut that I could trust him. I knew that he would immediately stop if I asked him to, and he let himself be guided by me. That is not to say the same will apply for everyone. If you were assaulted by someone you trusted, this may be a completely different situation. Ultimately, you must learn to trust yourself again before you can trust your partner, and that requires time and patience. But you will get there.

After the assault, I slowly reintroduced dates, at a pace that felt comfortable to me. I mean, sure, I was still working stupidly long law firm hours and so it wasn't always easy to fit them in, but I made a point of it, just to keep up my mischief, if nothing else. I explored my new boundaries, which over time started to fade away.

Once I had faced my worst nightmare, everything else fell into perspective. I realised there were so many insignificant things holding me back from living my fullest potential, be it fear of looking stupid, worry of what people might think of me, or fear of rejection. (That last one I still struggle with at times, by the way, so if I'm laughing loudly at all your terrible 'dad jokes' and keep making excuses to touch your arm, that's your cue to ask me out, please.) My romantic connections are deeper and more meaningful now, even the short ones, because I have to instinctively trust that person to be intimate with them. Placing your trust into the hands of someone else is intoxicating. I feel more confident. I move with intention and communicate better. I am less afraid of honouring my standards, and my demand for the utmost respect both ways is non-negotiable.

For both survivors and partners, it is essential to be very clear about desires and boundaries (which should be the case all the time, to be honest, and it doesn't have to be awkward or kill the mood, either). Talking about consent is sexy. It shows that you're comfortable in your own skin, that you know what you like and that you want both of you to have a good time. So don't be afraid to ask your partner what they are into, or if they are enjoying what you are doing.

* * *

What I'm saying, dear reader, is that as daunting as the path ahead seems, there really is a light at the end of it. Whether you are friend, family member, colleague or partner, it is not an easy route to navigate, mistakes will be made, and that's OK. You are dealing with an incredibly vulnerable person, but they're not made of glass either. It takes phenomenal strength to walk through fire like that and still be a functioning human on the other side.

If you choose to walk some of that path with them, you have an opportunity to be a part of their growing and flourishing garden. You are the ramparts and fortifications behind which the survivor can find their markers again. You are the first line of defence against the salt and salt-bearers. You have the amazing ability to create a sandbox for the survivor to experiment with their new reality – a place of embrace where shame and PTSD cannot fester. In that safe environment, you are helping them set the scene for their healing.

SURVIVAL GUIDE: ADVICE FOR THE SURVIVOR'S SUPPORT NETWORK

I haven't revealed anything particularly mind-blowing in this chapter. Most are things that are in the realm of common sense once you've heard them but, unfortunately, they are not things that are explained or spoken of nearly enough. The common denominator to all of them is that you, the supporter, are the survivor's link from the Shadowland back to reality.

I am listing here the things I wish people around me knew at the time, and the things they were probably too afraid to ask. No matter how afraid or unsure you may feel, I can guarantee you that the survivor is a hundred times more terrified. As long as you're showing up for the survivor, you're doing great.

Listen: there is a real art to being a good listener, and it's something we all need to work on. Trauma of this scale will be difficult to communicate for the survivor, so give them time, listen without interruption and be comfortable in silences while they gather their thoughts. Make eye contact when they speak. Don't be afraid to ask them questions or explain that you want to help them. When responding, build on what the person has said to you rather than what you think you should say.

Remember each survivor is unique: put your preconceived notions and ideas in a box, and burn it. I can guarantee you, whatever you think you know, chances are it won't apply here. Unless you have endured that kind of trauma it will be near impossible to understand, and even if you have, each person processes trauma differently. We all need and want different things, so assume you know nothing and keep an open mind.

Speak up: words matter. What matters even more is the fact that you are welcoming a dialogue. If you don't know what to say, try saying: 'You are so strong', 'I can't find the words to describe how brave you are', 'I have so much admiration for you', 'I hope you know how loved you are'. If you're worried or unsure about how to start the conversation, you can open with, 'I hope you don't mind me saying this' or 'I hope it's OK to say this ...'

Actions speak even louder than words: if you really cannot find the right words, particularly if you are not close to the survivor, at least make a point of making eye contact, smiling, being present. I understand wanting to give someone space, but do not avoid or withdraw from the person. I promise you, they feel isolated enough as is. Gently draw them back into the fold by regularly checking in, offering to go for a walk or dropping them a coffee once in a while. You have no idea what a difference that could make to someone who is really struggling.

Take the initiative: do not leave it to the survivor to reach out to you. Send the text, and not just the one, even if you don't get a response. Call them every now and then. If you don't know what to say, try saying, 'I was just thinking of you. I hope you're OK and I'm here if you're not.'

Understand the Fight, Flight, Freeze or Fawn responses to trauma: read up on these in Chapter 1 and be prepared to comfort a survivor if you hear them blame themselves for how they reacted during the assault.

Remind them they are safe: particularly in the immediate aftermath of the assault, or for someone who has PTSD. Their inner alarm bells may still be ringing loudly despite the danger having passed. You can help reinforce the internal work they are doing by gently reminding them that they are safe now, and that they are a survivor, not a victim.

Be mindful of your body language around them: watch their response and how their body language responds to yours. They may be triggered by aggressive posturing, knuckle cracking, a raised voice. If they seem to flinch at something, avoid doing it.

Let the survivor keep their sense of control, particularly in the first few weeks after the assault: let them touch you first. Let them come to you. For example, if you want to hug them, open your arms slowly but let them lead or close in. Let yourself be guided by them. You'll pick up quite quickly what they're comfortable with and then you can take it from there.

If you don't know, ask: what are their boundaries? Ask. Is it OK to say something? Ask. There is no such thing as a 'wrong' question if the place it comes from is one of good intentions. You can open with, 'I just want to make sure I'm not making you uncomfortable', or 'I am trying to understand what works best for you'. Keeping the lines of communication open is critical to keeping that person engaged and feeling supported.

You don't have to apologise: the instinctive reaction when someone shares something awful is to say, 'I'm so sorry'. Of course, there is no wrong thing to say, any words will be appreciated, but sometimes an apology can add to the weight of the survivor's guilt or shame. If you want to build a more empowering narrative, try phrasing your reaction in a positive light. Tell them they are strong or thank them for opening up (see below).

'Thank you for sharing that with me': when a survivor shares their story with you, no matter how you feel about it, thank them. Speaking up about something so private and vulnerable is a huge feat for them and they are honouring you by sharing it with you. It's also a great place-holder if you're caught off-guard and need to gather your thoughts.

Do not be afraid: or at least, try to avoid showing fear. Meet their gaze. Normalise the conversation around this. No rape victim is going to be triggered if you use the words 'rape' or 'sexual assault', particularly if you are being gentle and compassionate. Asking questions is a great way to show that you are not afraid to connect with the survivor and their experience, despite what has happened. It is empowering. You can start by saying, 'I hope you don't mind me asking ...' or 'I'm not sure if this is OK to ask, so please tell me if it isn't'.

If you are the survivor's employer, you have an extra layer of responsibility: check in regularly and don't simply ask them what they need. Instead, make tangible offers, such as do they need to take an afternoon off here or there if they get overwhelmed? Do they need to talk to someone in the firm or from any employee assistance programme? Reassure them about their job and tell them they're doing great when they are. Show them you care.

Acknowledge that you are going to get it wrong: this is inevitable. What works with me may not work with another survivor, and that's OK. We are human, we are not perfect. What matters is that you are trying, you are showing up and you are accepting wherever the survivor is on their journey.

Take onboard constructive criticism: if you do something that does not work, try not to get defensive when the survivor points this out to you. It is likely difficult for them to voice this with you rather than withdraw from you entirely. You can receive such interactions with words like, 'Thank you for telling me'. Don't be afraid to ask questions about how you can help them on their healing journey.

Get support: supporting a survivor can be a lot to deal with, particularly if they are family. Just like the survivor, you need to get the right supports in place for you. The organisations that offer support to survivors will often also help you as well, including the Dublin Rape Crisis Centre. See the Survival Guide at the end of Chapter 4 for details.

7.

Drum-roll: The Pre-trial Preparations

Diary entry, 18 November 2019:
'I'm tired of fighting. I can't do this anymore.'

The lead-up to the trial is excruciating, triggering some severe relapses of my PTSD and anger. The date is set for 7 December 2020. As the summer months faded away and we entered autumn, I could taste how real it was getting. The anxiety of not knowing what to expect, despite having asked a hundred questions to the gardaí and Prosecution about the process, the fear that I would screw up giving evidence, the terror of seeing Beast in court and putting a face to my nightmares, all culminated in extreme insomnia, constant nausea, migraines and panic attacks. On top of that, the COVID-19 pandemic meant it would not be safe for my parents to travel to Ireland, a heartbreaking sacrifice to have to accept. I had spent the last year thinking they would be by my side, and I couldn't imagine not having them there with me.

Preparations for the trial intensified in October, with weekly meetings with the gardaí, the Director of Public Prosecutions (DPP), Prosecution counsel and the Rape Crisis Centre. Regular calls with my office to keep them updated on developments. Intensified counselling sessions just to get through the brunt of it. I kept working full-time throughout it all. In hindsight, again, completely tapped. I was extremely lucky to be on a client secondment at the time, and the client and her team were the most supportive people I have ever had the pleasure of working with. I could not have done it in any other environment. If you can, I would highly recommend taking time off work in this period, or at least carving out time after each meeting to recover because they are so depleting.

Five weeks before the trial was due to start, it became clear at one of these meetings with Prosecution that despite having been assured from the start that there were 'special measures' in place to protect me from having to see Beast at the trial, nothing had been done about it. For over a year. I knew from my criminal law studies that victims could give evidence by video-link in sexual offence cases. It was bluntly pointed out to me, however, that this only applied to 'vulnerable witnesses', i.e. victims under eighteen years old or with a mental disorder. When no alternative was suggested, I asked about giving evidence behind a partition screen, which is another special measure available under Irish law. This was eventually agreed to, but I was required to complete a Vulnerability Assessment, an interview with An Garda Síochána to assess the victim's protection needs. The gardaí then submit a report to the DPP, which *may* apply for special measures at trial, 'if necessary'. Our justice system is so perverted that the *rape victim* has to *prove* that she (or he, or they) is vulnerable and will be retraumatised if made to face the accused while recounting the unspeakable violation inflicted by that person. That should be a given from the very fact of being a rape victim.

During this interview, you must give a detailed 'honest, vulnerable account' and prove that you have a 'particular vulnerability' to 'secondary and repeat victimisation, intimidation and retaliation' by the accused – meaning one single instance of intimidation or victimisation is not sufficient. The assessment takes into account the type, nature and severity of the offence, as well as whether you have suffered 'considerable harm' due to the offence. It's not a yes or no assessment, but rather 'to what extent' you require protection. The judge will have to balance your protection needs against the accused's right to a fair trial because, apparently, a small curtain of fabric between the two of you hinders that. Now, that's a lot of goddamn hoops to jump through, particularly when you then see the pathetic little structure being wheeled in at trial (more on that in Chapter 8).

My two cents on the Vulnerability Assessment – focus on how you would be unable to properly testify without this protection, which would thereby deny the judge and jury the key evidence they need to decide the case. Explain *why* this is so, in detail. Do you have PTSD? What are the symptoms? Has the accused threatened you or intimidated you before? Was the assault violent? If the accused is known to you, does he or she have body language or gestures that could be a disguised threat to you or a look that could destabilise you when you are giving evidence?

During the thirty-minute interview, I explain not only how seeing Beast would traumatise me by making me relive the assault but also, and more importantly, that I am terrified of him seeing me. This is a man who chased me twice when I was trying to get away. He is clearly dangerous and persistent. Right now, we don't know what each other looks like, but if I am forced to face him, I will lose that security of him not knowing my face. I will spend the rest of my life looking over my shoulder in fear. By the end of the interview, my voice is breaking and my face is drained of colour. I ask them to take a note of my state, too, and to record that this was my reaction to just *thinking* about giving evidence without the partition screen.

After the assessment, there was an agonising five-week wait because the ruling on the screen is only made on the day the trial starts, which defies all reason. This is something that should be decided well in advance, so that everyone can prepare themselves for what happens on the day, not just the victim but the accused as well. I was also told that there are only one or two of these screens in the country, therefore it has to be secured in advance to ensure it isn't in some courtroom in Limerick if your trial is taking place in Dublin. Moronic.

* * *

The greatest blow of all came in November, barely a fortnight before the trial was set to commence. Alison and I are due to fly from France on 22 November to quarantine in Dublin for two weeks, but on Wednesday, four days before our flight, I get a call from John, my Family Liaison Officer (FLO). He explains that two other cases are listed ahead of ours on the same day, and that they will be given priority because they involve juveniles. There aren't enough judges to hear all three cases, so unless the juveniles plead guilty, our case will not be going ahead in December.

'But for over a *year* I kept being told we had priority because the accused wasn't granted bail.'

As Beast is not an Irish national and has no fixed abode, he is considered a flight risk. That combined with the violence and severity of the offence meant he was not granted bail, so he has been remanded in custody for the past fifteen months. People in pre-trial detention are usually given priority ahead of people on bail because of the restriction on their personal liberty.

'I know,' John replies, 'but these two cases have higher priority because they're juvies. So as there's a high chance that your case won't be proceeding, the judge has decided to push the date back now.'

'But surely that's *my* decision, if I want to take that risk? Did nobody fight him on this? Is there anything I can do to change his mind?'

'I'm so sorry, Sarah. It's done. The judge has made his ruling.'

'I don't understand, John, surely the DPP's office knew about these other two cases? Mine has been listed for over a year, so it must be the same with these other two? How could they tell us that we had priority this whole time if they knew that we didn't?'

'I'm so sorry. The new trial date has been set for November 2021.'

My phone is on speaker and I hear my dad inhale sharply behind me. That statement is an atomic bomb. I'm speechless for a minute.

'But that's a *year*, John?!'

'I know. There's a backlog due to Covid so the delays are getting worse. All I can say is, I'm so sorry.'

I hang up the phone and fall apart. A year. A YEAR. We were so close. How can they throw a curveball like this so close to trial? It's inhumane. My parents, who always know exactly what to say, are at a loss for words. They just stand there, helpless. There is nothing to say.

For the two days that follow, I am in a state of extreme depression. All I can do is sit on my bed, spiritless, and cry silent tears of fury into the arms of my mom and dad. It's the first time I truly feel like giving up.

'I'm so angry.' I speak softly through the tears because I have actually reached my limit.

Eventually my dad, the eternal problem-solver, gently urges me to get the DPP to change the judge's mind. I tell him it's hopeless, we heard what John said about the ruling. And yet, he persuades me, I have to try. If we don't go ahead, it won't be for my lack of persisting. I did not come all this way to back down now.

That afternoon, I send an email begging the DPP to make the judge reconsider. I tell them I'm willing to come to Ireland at my own expense. I'm willing to quarantine and take the risk of the juveniles not pleading guilty on the day, just in case there is a chance that they do. I explain that the emotional and psychological effort it has taken to get here has been too great, and that I will not have the strength to muster it a second time.

My diary entry the next morning reads:

'I didn't sleep. It's impossible to close my eyes, but I don't have the energy to do anything. It's an effort even to breathe. The only thing I feel is extreme pain. A heaviness is crushing down on my chest. I feel so broken. No one is listening to me, not even the system that is supposed to protect me. I can't keep going, I just can't do this anymore.'

On Friday afternoon, we get a call from John. His voice is triumphant.

'You did it. We're back on for the seventh of December. Well done.'

I can't process the information. It's too much of an emotional roller-coaster. It's also Schrödinger's trial right now: it both is and isn't going ahead. We won't know until the day whether the juveniles are pleading guilty, which means our trial could still be delayed. And by then, the November 2021 slot could be gone and the delay could be far more than a year.

The next two days are a blur of packing, booking flights and accommodation.

We land in Dublin on the Sunday and go straight to our hotel to quarantine per COVID-19 protocols. Locked away in tiny living quarters for two excruciating weeks, there are not two, but three of us in the room. My sister, me, and my anxiety, which by now has mushroomed to the size and weight of a horse sitting on my constricted chest. We are trapped with this monster, who throws tantrums in the form of panic attacks at the smallest sensory triggers. Every day, we half-joke about how the tension in the room could not possibly get worse, and yet each following day we feel the pressure rise further. I am hypersensitive to scents and smells, to the point where I could whiff out anyone approaching our door from the other side of the corridor. The most random smells morph into alarm bells in my head that something is seriously wrong – kale in the mini-fridge (still wrapped in its airtight packaging, I might add), Alison's perfume, a couple of drops of coffee dried at the bottom of a mug. Every time I detect a new smell, I become extremely agitated and panicky for hours, obsessively trying to find a way to remove it from the air long after Alison had cleared away the offending item.

It isn't just smells, it's sounds too. The stress is so high that even the sound of a page turning can send me into a panic attack, which is unfortunate because both of us are working full-time during this self-isolation – me on my job, Alison on her mid-term university assignments. As if exams weren't stressful enough without being trapped in a room with a hyperventilating maniac and a rape trial hanging over your head. I exercise compulsively at every break I take (we're talking weighted planks and lunges with a suitcase propped up on my back), to relieve a sliver of the stress trapped in my body.

Some days I get triggered by even the sound of Alison's breathing. Ever accommodating and unwavering, she does not hesitate to hold her breath when tiptoeing around me. Multiple diary entries read, *'The anxiety is so bad I feel like peeling my own skin off and jumping out of it. There is no respite'.* What Alison was put through in that month, not only the trial, which was equally traumatic for her, but also the nerve-racking lead-up to it was, for a long time, something I thought I would never forgive the Irish courts for. I don't know how she did it.

* * *

That agonising two-week period was only a taster of what is to come, which I'll turn to in Chapter 8. Before I do, I want to talk to you a little about our criminal justice process generally and give you a word of warning on what lies ahead.

The trial was, hands down, the worst experience of my life. Far, far worse than the assault. It brought me to my knees, literally. I say this not to scare you, or to try to dissuade you from going down this route if that is what you want, but to make sure that you are walking into this with your eyes wide open. I would never tell anyone not to seek justice. That is something you, and only you, must decide. But the process is brutal. Now that my case is over, I don't regret having gone through with it, but my mettle had never been tested like that before. It took every ounce of resilience I had and then some, not to mention the unstinting support of some absolute heroes in my family, starting with Alison.

I'm very conscious here that, for many, trial will never be an option. For some, the crime may have been impossible to report, for any number of reasons; for others, the decision was taken away from them because there was not enough evidence or the DPP declined to prosecute. I cannot imagine what that feels like, nor do I pretend to understand. If you never make it to court, I hope you find some comfort in knowing that you have spared yourself a great deal of agony and heartbreak.

For those who do press ahead with a trial, all I can say to you is that our criminal courts may not be the white knight you want them to be. They can inflict an infinite amount of pain in the process of administering 'justice'. After exposing your deepest hurt and putting you through deep humiliation and intrusion that retraumatises you all over again, in a process that lasts for years and during which you are entirely powerless, you *might*, if you are lucky, get the verdict you hoped for. I did and, personally speaking, the case itself brought me very little closure. If it had only affected me, I would have walked away. The only thing that kept me going was the thought that Beast would do the same thing, or worse, to another woman, and I could not live with myself knowing I had let that happen.

The trial took over a huge part of my life. There have always been issues with delays and inefficiencies in the courts, but for crimes with such a fundamental impact on people's lives, years of waiting for a verdict is an outright denial of justice. From the day the date was set, almost eighteen months after the assault, I was unable to move forward with my life until that chapter was closed. And yet, eighteen months, I'm told, is record speed. Most rape and sexual assault cases take, on average, two to three years just for trial to be set, and that's assuming there are no adjournments (which there almost inevitably are). Having come through it, however, I can tell you that the ordeal does end, and that there is life and joy on the other side.

The first thing you hear when studying criminal procedure in law school is that the Irish system is 'very victim-friendly' and 'non-adversarial'. That could not be further from the truth. For starters, you, the victim, are not a victim in the eyes of the law. You are a witness to the crime (yes, you read that right). A crime that has been committed not against you, but against society at large. Therefore, the DPP is suing not on behalf of you, but on behalf of the people of Ireland. Consequently, you are not entitled to any legal representation. As a witness, you are not allowed to be prepared for trial by the Prosecution in any way that would amount to 'victim coaching', which means you are walking into court completely blind, not to mention alone.

Meanwhile, the Defence are twenty steps ahead of you at all times. They know the system inside-out, they may have pored over your counselling records and statement made to the gardaí, they have calculated their every move and they will employ disgraceful tactics that should, in my personal opinion, be criminalised. You are not walking into a fair fight.

So I am here to arm you with every weapon in my arsenal, and help you feel as ready as humanly possible to go in there and stand up for yourself, because nobody else is going to do it for you. And as we all know, the greatest weapon is knowledge. If you know what to expect and have visibility on what lies ahead, that is a huge variable ruled out of the list of things you have to worry about. You can then focus your entire attention on yourself and keeping your head above water. So let me run you through what happens in a court case, and let's get you armoured up for battle.

SURVIVAL GUIDE: THE PRE-TRIAL PREPARATIONS

Right, people, we are lawyering up. I know you feel vulnerable and afraid, you have every right to be. This is incredibly daunting and likely to be completely new territory for you. Have faith in yourself that you can do this. The Survival Guides in this chapter and the next, as well as the timeline and terminology sections below, are designed to give you a head-start on the trial and prepare you for the whole process. Let's give these people a run for their money.

Do not underestimate the time involved in the lead-up to trial: there
   will be increased meetings with the gardaí, your court accompanier,
   your counsellor and/or the DPP and Prosecution counsel. As you get
   closer to the trial, it will start to feel more real and each meeting will
   be draining. Take some time off work, if you can. Speak with your
   employer. You should be entitled to some compassionate leave (or even
   stress leave) if they are being difficult. Carve out some you-time to
   recover after each meeting.

Watch out for PTSD relapses: a trial is a huge source of stress and
   uncertainty, so it is only normal that you might feel triggered as you
   approach the date. Get your necessary supports in place a couple of
   months in advance to prepare yourself, especially therapy. (See Chapter
   4 for how to protect your counselling records.)

Ask for any special measures early on and keep asking: these are measures like getting a screen between you and the accused in court or

giving evidence by video-link. Put all of your requests to An Garda and the DPP in writing (email), and don't assume it will get done because the criminal courts system is highly inefficient and things get forgotten all the time. You have to be prepared to take it on yourself to keep applying pressure, so you may want to line up a support person for yourself, like a family member, who can help you through this.

When applying for protection measures, write down all the reasons why you need them: no detail is too small, you need to throw the kitchen sink at these people for them to take your request seriously. After the Vulnerability Assessment, follow up by email and send your list of reasons to ensure absolutely everything has been captured.

Ask about the legal jargon: the gardaí, the Defence and the Prosecution will probably throw around a lot of legal terms and words that you don't understand. I struggled to follow at times and I have a Law degree. Always ask them to explain it to you in plain English. (I've given you a head-start with the Terminology section below.)

Pick out what to wear at the trial: I know it sounds stupid, but appearances matter, and you have a jury of twelve people to get on your side. You don't have to wear a suit or heels, but I'd advise you to dress formally. Wear something that makes you feel comfortable and confident. I picked a long, black dress with a high neck and I wore it like armour. Have a couple of outfits lined up so you don't have to worry about a wardrobe malfunction on the day.

Just because you can't have legal representation doesn't mean you can't get legal advice: heartbreakingly, I only found out about this after the trial. If you are a victim of rape, aggravated sexual assault or incest, you are entitled to free legal advice from the Legal Aid Board (www. legalaidboard.ie/). This can be extremely useful if you want to get advice generally on the case ahead or on your counselling records. You can ask all your legal questions and get more detailed and satisfactory answers than the ones provided by the criminal justice system.

Read your statement ahead of the trial: the gardaí should give you a copy of this a week ahead of the trial. If they don't, ask them for it. Read it a couple of times, at least a few days before the trial, to refresh your memory. This is the main document on which you will be asked questions by the Prosecution and the Defence.

Remember the jury don't see your witness statement: the statement you give to the gardaí is not evidence presented at trial. Only your oral testimony given in court forms part of the evidence on which the crime is tried. Assume the jury know nothing.

Write down the key points to your story and practice it a few times with a friend: you definitely don't want to sound over-rehearsed but going through the story a couple of times might help you build 'memory muscle' around it and feel a little more confident.

Do not worry about blanking on the day: you will not have to tell the whole story from the top. Prosecution will go first and will guide you through your statement by asking you questions in the chronological order of your statement, working through the events as they occurred. If you forget something, they will prompt you, you don't have to worry about blanking on a part of your story.

LEGAL TERMINOLOGY

Even as a lawyer, I struggled to keep up with all the lingo and legal terms that the DPP, the Prosecution and the gardaí throw around in court. Below are some of the fundamental terms you ought to know ahead of proceedings commencing, to better understand what will happen at trial.

Bail: the accused can be released on bail after they have been charged. Conditions often apply (e.g. lodging monies as a guarantee they will appear in court, etc.). The opposite of being granted bail is called being **'remanded in custody'** (taken to prison) until trial.

Beyond reasonable doubt: you might hear this often during the trial. This is the 'threshold' or standard of proof that the Prosecution must meet to prove their case. The jury must find that the evidence presented proves the accused is guilty beyond reasonable doubt, i.e. it is not a mathematical certainty, but beyond likely or probable that he or she committed that offence. If there is a real doubt (as opposed to a whim) in the jury's mind, they must find the accused innocent.

Book of Evidence: a folder containing all the evidence that the Prosecution intends to rely on in trial to prove the accused committed the crime (including forensic photographs, witness statements, etc.). Witnesses and victims are not given a copy of this Book, they only have access to their own statement. Only the Prosecution, the Defence and the accused have access to the full Book.

Counsel: another word for lawyer (usually it means the barristers, but in some cases it can refer to solicitors). Both the Prosecution and Defence teams usually have a senior counsel, who leads the case, and a junior counsel.

Cross-examination: the formal interrogation of a witness by Defence once that person has been questioned (or '**examined**') by the Prosecution. The point of cross-examining a witness is to challenge or highlight the weaknesses in that witness's account, and so to undermine the opposing party's evidence.

Fair trial: any person to be tried on a criminal charge is guaranteed a fair trial by Article 38.1 of the Irish Constitution. This right covers a wide rake of sub-rights, including the right to due process, the right to be heard, the right to legal defence, the presumption of innocence until proven guilty (by a jury save in exceptional circumstances), and the right to cross-examine any evidence presented by the Prosecution, to name but a few.

In camera: a trial being heard *in camera* means in private. All sexual offences cases are heard *in camera*. No members of the public are allowed in the courtroom. However, members of the press can be present to report on the case without naming you (more on this in Chapter 9).

Indictment: this means either (a) the formal document setting out the charge(s) against the accused or (b) the formal reading of those charges to the accused on the first day of trial. The accused must '**plead**' guilty (in which case the trial commences) or not guilty (in which case a date is set for sentencing) to the indictment.

Swear in: witnesses and jurors must be '**sworn in**', meaning they must either swear an **oath** on a holy book or '**affirm**' that (1) the evidence they will give is true (for witnesses), or (2) that they will try the issues and return a true verdict based on the evidence (for jurors).

Witness vs victim: astonishingly, victims of rape and sexual assault in Ireland are still legally defined as 'complainants', which have the status of witnesses for the purpose of the trial. This means they are not afforded legal representation in court save in exceptional circumstances (e.g. if Defence want to bring in the victim's sexual history as an argument). However, they are still entitled to legal advice on the case (which was not made clear to me, so a good one to note). All victims of rape and serious sexual assault can get free legal aid from the Legal Aid Board (www.legalaidboard.ie) (more on this in the Survival Guide above).

TIMELINE OF A COURT CASE

The lead-up to trial can be extremely stressful. I find one way to combat the nerves is to inform yourself on what to expect. Below is a very general timeline to give you a sense of what's ahead. On average, a rape trial can last one to two weeks, but remember that trials are unpredictable so this can vary hugely. There is more detail in Chapter 8 on my case to give you a flavour of Defence tactics and practical considerations like court accompaniers or how to prepare yourself mentally.

Commencement of trial – the first day of trial will be the date listed on the court summons you were given by the gardaí (the document noting the name of the offender, the offences he/she is charged with).

Jury selection: a pool of jurors is selected at random for a particular case. Prosecution and Defence then ask each juror a couple of questions and can 'challenge' (reject) up to seven prospective jurors each, without giving a reason. This is very common, so don't panic if it happens. After twelve jurors are chosen, they are each sworn in, meaning they swear they will return a true verdict based on the evidence. This whole process takes about an hour. You cannot be present (as you have not yet given your evidence), but your accompanier or a friend can go down for you, if you want them to.

Indictment and Opening statements: once the jury, judge presiding and accused are all seated, the indictment – a summary of the charge(s) against the accused – is formally read out. The accused will formally enter a plea (guilty or not guilty) at this stage. If the plea is 'not guilty', Prosecution (and sometimes Defence) will move on to their opening speech, introducing the facts and explaining what evidence they are going to rely on.

Evidence: witnesses and experts are then called to give evidence. They are questioned by Prosecution first (sometimes called 'examination in chief'), then cross-examined by Defence. This usually follows the order outlined below, but this can vary depending on what counsel decide, or if someone is late, for example. Typically, the evidence takes a number of days, at least, to get through.

- **Mapping garda:** the first person called is normally the garda who photographed the crime scene. They will set the scene for the jury, show them maps of where the assault or rape happened, and photos taken by Forensics.

- **Injured parties:** this will usually start with you, the victim, as you are the most important 'witness'. If there were other injured parties or any witnesses, they will be called up after you. (More detailed advice on giving your evidence is given in the Survival Guide to Chapter 8.)

- **Technical evidence:** this will include the gardaí you gave the statement to and any doctor or medical practitioner who gathered medical evidence (i.e. anyone at SATU or hospital). Their evidence is much more technical. They will cover not only their evidence but how they gathered it and if they followed the required procedures.

- **Defence witnesses:** after Prosecution has called up all their witnesses, Defence may call witnesses or present evidence, but they may choose not to, for example if there were no other witnesses present.

Legal arguments: once all the evidence has been presented, Prosecution and Defence move to present their legal arguments to the judge. The jury is not present during these. The judge will make a ruling on what arguments can be presented to the jury in the closing statements.

Closing statements: Prosecution and Defence then each make a speech summarising the evidence they are relying on and their legal arguments.

Charging the jury: after the closing statement, the judge will 'charge' the jury, meaning the judge will state the applicable law, explain in detail each component of the crime that the jury must decide applies, and then recap the facts. This can take some time, anywhere between two hours to two days, so be prepared to be patient.

The jury retires: the deliberations can take anything from one hour to ten days. The jury must reach a unanimous verdict on each of the charges, and they must consider all the evidence presented at trial.

Verdict: the jury reconvenes and is asked by the judge to give a 'guilty' or 'not guilty' verdict. Sometimes, the jury will be offered to find a 'lesser' charge (so for example in my case, the jury could have found a guilty verdict for sexual assault instead of aggravated sexual assault if they had found that the violence used by Beast was 'intended only to escape' and not to commit the actual assault).

Sentencing: after the verdict, the judge will set a date for sentencing (usually four to five weeks later). This will give you time to write your Victim Impact Statement (see Chapter 9), which you or someone you choose can read out at that hearing.

8.

Circus: The Trial

Diary entry, Monday, 7 December 2019:
'To war, we are going to war.'

It is the eve of the trial.

The rage of being made to wait until tomorrow to know if we're going ahead or living with this bullshit for another year, if I'll be made to see Beast, if I'll have to go through with my evidence or be spared by his guilty plea, it's enough to make anyone lose their mind. I need to do something, so I write down the key points I don't want to miss when giving my evidence and I rehearse my story with Alison a couple of times. We resist doing it more than that because the last thing you want is to sound over-rehearsed. You want to be as raw as possible for the jury.

Sleep does not come easy that night.

The next morning, I wake up to my heart pounding in my ears. My Fitbit displays 110 heartbeats per minute. That's impressive for someone who's been horizontal for seven hours. Checking my phone, I have a text from Nikki, my best friend in London, which gives me a little courage:

'This is a reminder that Monday 7 December 2020 only happens once. You

only have to go through this day once. No matter how today goes, even if it is very bad, you will never have to live through it again. You are strong and I know you can do this.'

We still don't know about the goddamn partition screen, so I pull my hair into a tight side-ponytail that I can hide behind my shoulder so Beast can't see the length of my hair. I do my make-up differently, too, contouring heavily so I look different from my usual self. Anything to make me less recognisable in case Beast sees me. The things victims must think about to protect themselves because they are failed by our justice system, it's despicable.

John collects Alison and me and drives us to the Criminal Courts of Justice (CCJ), just next to Dublin's beautiful Phoenix Park. The CCJ building is a glittering bastion, its 360-degree sawed-glass façade catching the morning sun like a crystal. Outside it, three legendary Irish heroines are waiting – Eileen, Erika and Kunak. My aunt and two cousins. They've driven from other counties to be here today, and I cannot put my gratitude into words when I see them. They join forces with Alison and I now have four kickass women worthy of a queen's guard by my side as we make our way into the CCJ. It's just as well, too, because it feels like we're marching into war, or to my execution, I can't quite tell.

Oh holy Lord Lantern Jaysus *Christ*, there are a lot of people in here. The ground floor hosts the lobby, jury reception and District Courts – basically for all minor offences, from dangerous driving to petty theft. It's milling with people in suits, Garda uniforms and tracksuits. John quickly guides us upstairs to the Central Criminal Court area (where the High Court exercises its criminal jurisdiction), and then up a further flight of stairs to the Victim Suite, a separate area for victims and their families to wait in, away from the hustle and bustle downstairs. There we meet Margaret, my accompanier from the Dublin Rape Crisis Centre. She's there to provide emotional and practical support regarding the court process.

While the antics downstairs are deciding on my fate, Margaret offers to take me to visit one of the empty courtrooms. This is crucial as it's important to get a feel for it, particularly if you have never been in court before. You want to see where you will walk in, where everything is, where to go and who to look at.

I'm trembling like a leaf entering the sombre, oppressive room. Margaret gets me to sit in the hot seat and shows me at what angle to turn the chair to avoid having Beast in my field of vision, should the unthinkable happen and the partition screen be denied. I shudder at the thought. She sits in the accused's box, to check that Beast can't see my long hair tucked behind my farthest shoulder. I'm horrified at how close the victim and the accused sit, mere feet away from each other. Margaret reminds me that Beast is allowed to stand and stretch while I speak – *WHAT?!* – and I should not let myself be thrown by that. *Sure, piece of cake.* His 'box' is only about waist-high, after that there is nothing but air between him and me. Nothing to stop him from reaching over and touching me, as I am well within arm's length. The way the room is laid out, he's slightly farther back than I am, meaning that if I'm facing the jury, the side and back of my neck are incredibly exposed. If we don't get this screen, I just won't be able to do it. I feel I'm going to be sick. Margaret interrupts my rising nausea with an additional layer of disquieting information, about the Defence this time.

'Just keep in mind, whatever they do, it's not personal. Rise above and try not to take it to heart.'

'Yeah, yeah. They're just doing their job and defending their client.'

'Not just that.'

'What do you mean?'

'They're not just defending their client, they are going to do everything to try to destabilise you. Particularly in a clear-cut case like this. It's their only way of winning.'

'But this isn't about *winning*. This is about finding out whether the law was broken and giving the accused a fair trial.'

'Just be aware that they have lots of tricks up their sleeves. They can try to confuse you and muddy the waters. Sometimes they get quite adversarial if they think it will disconcert you, because you're less likely to look credible if you're scrambling for words. Do not give them the time of day, stay calm. And it's not just tone, you know, it's also body language that may feel aggressive to you. They might put one foot up on the bench and lean towards you as they question you. Some barristers are renowned for it.'

'I'm sorry, *WHAT?*'

I have seen the peacocking type in the Four Courts before. Some of these gobshites will put their foot on the bench and manspread, in a standing lunge. It's revolting. One of my most satisfying work memories ever was participating in a watching brief and a female judge snapping at one of the barristers, asking him if he thought he was in his living room. I've never seen someone look like such a sheepish schoolboy.

'You're telling me that they pull that obscene posture at highly vulnerable, SEXUALLY TRAUMATISED rape victims? WHILE they are interrogating them?!'

Margaret nods solemnly.

'How can judges let them away with that?'

Rage rises. I actually hope the Defence barrister does try to pull that one now. I'll put him back in his box so fast he won't have time to blink. Spoiler alert, none of them did try it, but I was grateful to Margaret for the warning. Aggressive posturing is a known problem in the court system, and it's good to prepare yourself for it as it can really overwhelm when you're already in such a vulnerable state (more on this in the Survival Guide).

* * *

Back in the Victim Suite, it's a waiting game now. I'm getting more restless by the minute. The uncertainty is just killing me. Alison, Erika, Kunak and Eileen are doing everything they can to keep me distracted. They are perfection – they listen when I need to vent, they bring coffee and cake even when I say I don't want any, just so I can do something with my hands, they're just *there*. Poor John is doing laps of sprints up and down the stairs all morning between the courtroom and Victim Suite, in a full suit and tie too, to keep us updated on progress. My God, that man must have the physical stamina of a cheetah.

After an age, John comes back, escorted by the Prosecution team. They want to speak to me privately in a separate room. This can't be good news. Alison comes with me and we sit down, but they won't say a word until the door is closed. My heart is pounding as I clutch Alison's hand. One of us is shaking, I can't tell which. Maybe it's both of us. Then senior counsel speaks up.

'The trial is proceeding.'

I nearly faint. I can't take in one other word of what they're saying after that. I'm too busy trying to stop the tears of victory that have risen to my eyes from flooding down my face. Judging by Alison's power grip on my hand, so is she. After counsel is done, I can't help giving them a brazen look.

'I'm glad I pushed it.' I raise my eyebrows boldly to distract from my watery eyes.

'It's to your credit, Miss Grace. We would not be here today if it weren't for your tenacity.'

I feel so vindicated.

Back in the Victim Suite our family is waiting, hanging on our every word, but all I can muster is a 'we did it' before my face goes to pieces and I burst into tears. I think Alison and I just held each other for minutes on end, sobbing from the release. And we're half French, you know, the country that invented blasé. I'm not one for drama or theatrics. In fact, when it comes to the poker face, I've been accused on a number of occasions of being an ice queen. But that's the pressure-cooker of emotions you're dealing with when trying to stay on top of all these upheavals.

Now that trial is going ahead, we're free to go for the rest of the day. John explains that there's a lot of procedural administration now that we're starting, so the jury won't be picked tomorrow or Wednesday, we'll know this afternoon. Kunak drives us back to Erika's house to celebrate with pink prosecco and pizza on the balcony. We're all laughter and lightness. I'm calling friends and family to let them know the news. The Graces won. We're stubborn and strong-headed, we took on the system and we feckin' won. The smile on my face has not faded since we left court. I'm beyond euphoric. It feels like I'm floating, and not from dissociation for once. My entire body is buzzing. I've never felt elation like this in my life.

A call from John at 3.00pm pierces my blissful bubble. He sounds very uncomfortable.

'We have a problem.'

My heart sinks as he explains that Defence is now arguing that Beast is 'unfit to plead'. Apparently, he is being uncooperative with his counsel and not accepting their advice to plead guilty, so Defence are claiming that he does not have the intellectual capacity to comprehend the proceedings. This had already been assessed back in July, when he apparently pleaded not guilty, and he was found fit to plead then, but even still it's being brought up again now. Beast is to be examined by a doctor tomorrow and we'll have the results on Wednesday, but John explains that if he is found unfit to plead, the trial could be off again.

Sweet. Suffering. *CHRIST*. We're back to square one.

I'm breathing slowly, trying to make sense of this information, but I feel dizzy. Why the *hell* is this being raised now, when it's known that we flew over specifically for the trial and had to quarantine for two weeks? This is so out of the blue. Why could this not have been done two weeks ago? And if Beast is found unfit to be tried, can he be found fit again in a few months? Is it due to his low IQ, or is it based on insanity? What are the consequences of it? John is staggering under my avalanche of questions. I pull up my old criminal law student notes on my laptop. The section 4 application under the Criminal Law (Insanity) Act 2006 requires a finding of unfitness to be tried to be due to a *mental disorder*. No definition for that term. Even more alarming, the section provides that if an accused is found unfit to be tried, the court can discharge him if it is satisfied that there is a reasonable doubt as to whether he committed the alleged crime. That means he could walk away without a trial, and possibly be committed to an institution.

John says all we can do now is sit tight until Wednesday. I slump back into the sofa, deflated.

* * *

Tuesday is the longest day in history, and the evening is the worst of my entire life. That night broke me. The anxiety is unlike anything I have ever experienced. Alison and I try to distract ourselves as best we can, but the hours drag on, and by the evening I am a huddled mess on the floor, my lifeless back propped against the side of the bed.

Nikki was wrong, turns out there is more than one 7 December 2020. I cannot believe I have to be put through this ordeal a second time. The rage and heartbreak of being forced to relive that night are overtaken only by the feeling of sheer and utter helplessness. It's like waiting to find out about an execution. I am totally in the dark and at these clowns' mercy. I have no idea what crappy excuse might cause a delay next, and I have no way of preparing myself. I don't know if we're going ahead tomorrow. I don't know how long the delay could be. I don't know if the judge will agree to the screen, or if I will have to testify sitting next to that creature. I don't know if I'll be able to physically speak, or if I'll have a panic attack. It's mental torture. The physical pain from the anxiety and the rage is unbearable. My heart feels like it's ensnared in the jaws of a bear trap. I'm crippled from feeling sick to my stomach. I can't breathe. I have been sobbing for hours, waves of agony rocking through my shoulders. All I can seem to say between sobs is, 'It's too hard, I can't do this', over and over again. Alison gets my parents on the line from France, but they're as heartbroken and powerless as I am.

My dad sees red. 'Fuck these people, Sarah. I would have walked away a long time ago. Get on a plane and come home. You owe them absolutely nothing.'

'I can't. *I can't.* If I leave now, there is no case and Beast walks.'

I've never wailed in my life before. I am wailing now.

'I'm so *ANGRY*. How can the system treat people like this? It's supposed to be defending victims, not adding to their trauma. It's too much. It's just too much for one person. They have no idea what they're putting me through. It's inhumane. *I can't do this.*'

Tears of despair and rage are streaming down my face and neck to my collarbone.

'You're in the middle of a nightmare, Sarah.'

* * *

I get no sleep that night. I watch the luminous numbers on the hotel clock move at tormenting pace. After what seems like an aeon, it's finally 7.00am. My Fitbit is still displaying 110 heartbeats per minute. I'm beyond shattered, resigned and shell-shocked. The nausea is at an all-time high.

Walking towards the CCJ, I look up in quiet fury and will the whole place to go up in flames. *Damn you all to hell.* At the entrance, though, Erika is waiting for us. I didn't even have to text her. She knew, and she's here. Upstairs, outside the courtroom, a couple of the gardaí take one look at my ashen face and give us a sympathetic nod through clenched jaws.

'I know,' says one, 'it's a circus.'

I nod in response.

We wait in the Victim Suite and an hour later John bounds in with the news that the trial is proceeding. This time, I feel absolutely nothing. There is no relief. I just look at him impassively. It's a trick, it's just another trick. They're going to change their minds in an hour because Beast is wearing the wrong shade of purple or something. I am burnt out by this shit. I'll believe we're proceeding when I'm in the chair giving evidence, not one second before.

As we wait for things downstairs to kick off, I spend the morning venting to Alison, Erika and Sheila, my other aunt who came in for today. I had no idea how appallingly rape victims were treated in this country. The torment I am being put through hardly seems worth it. There's more tears of rage and colourful language, but at least I'm getting it off my chest instead of letting it fester within. The three of them listen to me unwaveringly, until I eventually tire out.

The jury is picked that afternoon – eleven men and one woman. I'm panicked by this ratio, but Margaret reassures me this is good news. Supposedly, men are statistically more likely to convict than women are. Never heard that one before, but I take her word for it. Erika goes down to the courtroom for reconnaissance and comes back later that afternoon with a more detailed report than the entire criminal justice staff have given me so far, combined.

'It's really tense down there. They read the charges to the jury, which sound really bad. Especially the aggravated sexual assault charge because it involves "serious violence and injury or degradation". And then they explain it happened in your home during a burglary, which is even worse. When they summarised the facts, there were audible gasps in the jury. One of the jurors was whimpering 'Oh my God' under their breath, they looked really upset. I think they're as afraid as you are, Sarah.'

That really helps.

'And Sarah – *him*. Beast, I mean. You have nothing to be afraid of. I know you're scared. I was really nervous going in because I didn't know what my reaction was going to be. But he's not intimidating at all. If anything, I don't think he fully gets what's going on. He looks really bored, despite the serious atmosphere, which is not doing him any favours. It's almost offensive. He's half hiding his face behind his hands and he isn't looking at anyone.'

That helps even more. At least now I can picture the scene I'm walking into tomorrow.

John comes back in at 4.00pm to release us for the day and to confirm that the judge has *finally* agreed to the screen. That's a huge relief. Although, again, I'm afraid to rely on this information. John explains that the judge took ages to reach his decision. Apparently, it's very rarely granted because it risks the accused looking guilty. (*Right*, because being flanked by gardaí doesn't do that?) Clearly, we have an issue in this country with allowing women to feel an ounce safer if it may adversely impact a man in any way. Supposedly, there has to be a whole ruling on balancing the victim's protection needs versus the accused's right to a fair trial because, in Ireland, you have the constitutional right to face your accuser. Having studied constitutional law, I animatedly point out to John that I never remember coming across that one. John patiently tries not to sigh. That man honestly deserves an award for putting up with my constant legal arguing. He explains that it's implied as part of the wider constitutional right to due process. Either way, he says, the screen will be there tomorrow, and that's what counts.

That night, although it feels like I have to go through the eve of the trial for a third time, I know we've made progress. This time, I know it's going ahead. I also know I have the screen, which is an enormous relief. I go through my evidence with Alison a couple of times again before bed and miraculously get some much-needed sleep.

* * *

Thursday is D-Day. I wake up to my Fitbit angrily flashing 120 heartbeats per minute. If we keep going at this rate, I'm going to need a cardiologist. My stress has reached a whole new level, including an angry stress rash on my neck and jaw. It's different from the uncertainty of not knowing if we're going ahead. Now it feels like the most important exam of my life. *Don't screw this up, Sarah. Do not let the women of Ireland down.* I do my hair and make-up normally because I don't need to hide from Beast anymore. I don my armour – long black dress with a high collar and comfortable black ankle boots. I feel powerful, but the heel on the boots is low enough that I can run away if Beast tries to come at me through the screen.

In the Victim Suite, I pace up and down the room incessantly. Erika is in the courtroom, watching the first expert witnesses called up. They are the gardaí who met us at the taxi and the mapping garda, who will take the jury through the layout of the crime scene. Kunak knows exactly what to say to calm me down.

'There is no way you can screw this up, Sarah.'

'But what if I blank? I can't remember my notes.'

'You won't blank. I'm sure the barrister will prompt you.'

The court breaks for lunch, but I can't touch a bite. I'm up first thing in the afternoon. We go for a power walk in the Phoenix Park to bring my anxiety down a notch, but it's still through the roof. I want to impale myself on the Wellington obelisk. I've decided I don't want anyone from my family in the courtroom when I testify. I need to focus on the jury and nothing else. I've agreed to Margaret being there, as she's more removed and won't be upset at the gruesome details or offensive questioning.

* * *

John comes to get me at 1.00pm.

'It's time.'

Execution time. Let's pray for a reprieve.

John has to bring me down early because I will be entering via the judge's chambers at the back of the courtroom. I cannot walk in through the normal entrance or Beast would see me, which would defeat the whole purpose of the screen. We walk into the now empty courtroom and there's a gathering of half-a-dozen gardaí at the end of the room, curiously milling around something. As we approach, clear disappointment is registered on their faces. They're muttering to each other, 'This is it?'

John and I ask what the commotion is about.

'This is the screen. I've never seen one before. I was expecting something … bigger.'

I look down at the sad little contraption. For all the drama about vulnerability assessments and the accused looking guilty, I was expecting some large structure to be erected through vigorous manpower. This is a foldable projector screen. Three pieces of aluminium propping up a square of thin black and grey fabric, no bigger than three feet wide. Talk about making a mountain out of a molehill.

John shows me how to walk in from the judge's chambers without Beast seeing me. The screen is stupidly narrow, so I have to unceremoniously crab-walk around the judge and the clerks, with my back pressed firmly to the wall, in order to remain hidden by the screen at all times until I sit down. The gardaí have me sit in the chair to test the screen, and that's when we realise there's a new issue: half the jury can't see me. We try different angles until eventually they tell me to just perch at the edge of the chair. *Man*, this has not been thought through.

The clerk then lets John and me into the judge's empty chambers. We have to wait there until the proceedings resume. We're told the running order has been changed. I will be brought in first, then Beast. Once we're all seated, the jury will then come in, otherwise, Beast would look guilty to the jury. *No shit, because nothing says guilty like a cowering victim sliding down the wall.* John sees the stress on my face and gives me a little pep-talk.

'All you can do now is take a deep breath and try to relax. This is your time to tell your story, so don't let anyone rush you. Just take your time. You'll be great. You're doing women a massive service by doing this.'

Literally the only reason I'm still here.

After twenty minutes, the clerk comes in to get me. *Showtime.* My heart is in my throat as I walk in. The courtroom looks so different now that it's full of clerks, security, gardaí and other staff. There are about twenty people here, and the jury aren't even in yet. I quickly sit into the chair, remove my COVID face mask and try to take a few deep breaths. I look up at the judge and he gives me a nod and a kind smile. I needed that – it's a world of relief.

We wait for minutes on end, in silence, before they bring in Beast. From the corner of my eye, I notice the judge staring at my hands. I look down and they are gripped so tightly together, my knuckles and fingers are white. And then I hear it. A noise to my right, from behind the screen, like a rasping breath. Beast. He is right next to me right now. Panic is shooting up my chest. My entire body has recoiled as far left in the chair as I can go, gripping the armrests and staring at the screen unblinkingly. I'm holding my breath for fear of making a sound. I try to channel Erika's words from yesterday: *he doesn't know what's going on. He probably doesn't speak much*

English, and he might even have no idea who is behind the screen. I try to settle back.

Finally, the jury minder brings in the jurors. They have to walk in four by four due to social distancing rules. As each wave comes in, they all stare at me. I can't hold their gaze and look down, but I can feel the weight of their curious eyes on me. This is the first time they are putting a face to the horror story they have just heard, and now they are about to hear it first-hand. This moment will decide if I am believed or not. I have never felt so vulnerable or exposed in my life. My still-clasped hands are shaking now and I feel my lip quiver. Oh no, no no no no no. *Not already.* I start crying uncontrollably. It's silent tears, but I can't stop. Lip still trembling, I clench my jaw and force myself to look up and lock eyes with the twelve strangers. Despite their face masks, their faces register a lot of different emotions – some fear, some curiosity, some apprehension, but also a lot of good will.

When it comes to swearing me in, my voice is breaking so much I can hardly get through it. *Deep breaths, Sarah, this is your time.* Counsel for Prosecution rises first, asks me a few questions about me, where I live and details of the apartment. He then guides me through what happened the evening before and then when I woke up. The narrative I've run through half-a-dozen times with Alison kicks in like muscle memory. I start telling my story earnestly, remembering Margaret's advice to talk to the jury, not to the barristers. I speak slowly, trying to remember that although this is my life story, this is the first time they are hearing it. I look at each of them in turn. As I speak, it strikes me that they are listening. I'm talking and people are *listening to me.* I not only have a captive audience but they are drinking in my words. For the first time in a long time, I feel heard. I start to get on a roll and keep going, almost uninterrupted by Prosecution.

Suddenly, I see something move in front of me. In the plastic COVID partition barrier between me and the law clerk directly in front of me, I see a reflection. It's Beast's hand. I freeze for a second, rooted to my chair. Mercifully, I can't see his face, but his arm and hand are in clear sight. I take a shaky but deep breath and continue. We have come too far to stop now. Finally, Prosecution asks their last question.

'Did you consent to this man assaulting you?'

'Absolutely not.'

'Thank you, no further questions.'

It feels like I have been talking for hours. My jaw hurts. I let myself slide slightly back into my chair as Defence gets up. Prosecution and Defence counsel apparently have to share a standing desk for all their paperwork, so I have a minute of respite while the awkward trading of the desk ceremony unfolds. Eventually, Defence is ready. I feel myself square my shoulders in anticipation. *Now for the hard part.*

The barrister catches me completely off-guard by starting with a long spiel on how he believes me, but it is his job to ask me these questions as he has to give his client a fair trial. I nod along cautiously. He then *apologises* for having to put me through these questions. This surely must be for the benefit of the jury, but I was not expecting this approach at all. I'm polite and respectful back to him – *two can play this game, my friend.*

He then puts his first question to me, asking if the intruder came into my room not knowing it was a bedroom. Before I know it, I have agreed that Beast did not know. *RATS.* I allowed myself to get lulled into a false sense of security by all his niceties and now I have testified to something I shouldn't have. In evidence, you should only speak to what you know. When asked about the accused's state of mind, I should clearly have said,

I don't know. *Well played, counsel, well played.* Right, that's my first and last mistake. For the rest of his questions, I watch my step, taking a few seconds each time to think it through fully before answering.

Throughout Defence's line of questioning, it becomes clear that the strategy is to prove that Beast's sole intention was to commit the burglary, not the aggravated sexual assault. *Yeah, sure, he tripped and fell fingers-first into her.* Defence asks me if the accused broke into my home with the intention of stealing from me. I wait for Prosecution to object. Nothing. Gotta do it myself, so.

'As you know, I can only speak to what I know. I cannot know what was going on in the accused's mind.'

How do you like them apples. I feel emboldened, I do. I think of all the survivors this bullshit was pulled on and I want to knock him down a peg (or five) for them. Defence asks the same question again, rephrased slightly. I look at Prosecution – still no objection. I give the same answer. Defence asks a third time but now the judge intervenes, sternly pointing out that I have already answered the question and to move on. The Sarah in my head is doing a victory lap of the courtroom.

Defence's line of questioning becomes stranger as we go on. They are clearly trying to muddy the waters around the facts to cast just enough of a reasonable doubt in the jury's minds. They put it to me that the accused did not know there were no men in the flat, and so perhaps he was simply stopping me from alerting a man who would fight him or prevent him from escaping. Again, I point out that I cannot speak to Beast's thoughts, however I do know that when trying to get away from him, he ran after me twice, and that is not the behaviour of someone trying to escape. Defence reads an excerpt from Beast's statement alleging that I attacked *him*, stopping him from getting away and violently ripping his T-shirt in the process. I admit that while I don't remember ripping his T-shirt, SATU found some of his blood under my fingernails from when I scratched him to defend myself, so it's possible that I did, but I note that *I* was the one who was prevented from escaping, not the other way around.

Finally, the questioning culminates in the most obnoxious argument I've ever heard. Defence latches on to the line in my statement on the violation being inflicted 'with the force of a punch'. He goes on to describe a boxer's jab and tries to insinuate that Beast's intention was not sexual but rather to hit me as retaliation for the thrashing I gave him. I remind him that my precise words were that the *violation* had 'the force of a punch', and last time I checked a boxer's jab is delivered with a closed fist, not an open hand. Defence puts it back to me that Beast did not intend the punch to land where it did because 'a punch isn't sexual'.

And there we have it, ladies and gentlemen. These are the pedantic lows to which our criminal justice system is willing to sink. Even in a case where the facts are so crystal clear-cut, we are still wasting valuable time (not to mention taxpayers' money) nit-picking on the choice of the victim's words spoken in the wake of a terrifying assault. A few of the jurors fold their arms at that last comment. I glare coolly at Defence and let the stupidity of those words sink in for a couple of seconds before responding, my voice icy.

'It felt pretty sexual to me.'

I see a couple of jurors nodding firmly in agreement behind him. *God, that is satisfying.*

After nearly two hours of questioning, Prosecution and Defence finally rest. The judge dismisses the jury, before Beast is taken away, and then I am at last allowed to take my leave. I lock eyes with a couple of gardaí at the other end of the room and they are beaming. They quietly whisper 'well done' as I walk past them on my way out. I smile weakly back. Words cannot describe the relief of it being over. I take a full breath for the first time in weeks.

My whole family is waiting outside, eyes huge with anticipation. They rush up to me and John as we step out of the courtroom. I nod once.

'They said you were incredible! John kept running in and out to tell us and the other gardaí how amazing you were doing.'

'I feel like it couldn't have gone better.'

John concurs. 'You did so well. You should be really proud of yourself.'

I feel vindicated. My obsessive note-taking and rehearsing the story with Alison really paid off. It goes to show how important your preparation is, not that anyone tells you that.

'How are you feeling, Sarah?'

Elated. High on adrenaline. On cloud nine. So relieved I could faint. I can't quite voice any of those emotions right now, though, so instead I go with, 'Apparently, when he was arrested, he complained that I ripped his T-shirt.'

Kunak's head falls back in laughter. 'You legend.'

I try and fail to hide a proud grin.

***

Prosecution counsel swing by the Victim Suite afterwards for a quick debrief. The 'dream witness', they say. I would like that framed. That has to be the only time a barrister has ever said that to a solicitor, because we're renowned brain-melters when it comes to testifying. I ask them about the rest of the proceedings. In November, they had advised that I should try to come into court daily, if possible, and sit in the audience for 'jury optics'. They said it was important for the jury to remember there is a victim (*cough* witness) involved here. I ask how that works seeing as we got the screen. I'll sit in if I absolutely have to, but we worked so hard to secure the screen between Beast and me on the basis that I was terrified of seeing him. Admittedly, it's very different having to sit next to him while giving evidence versus being half-hidden in the audience, but I can just see Defence jumping up and down and saying we deprived Beast of a fair trial if I *am* physically capable of being in his presence. I'm met with blank looks. No one has thought of that. They think about it, but don't see an issue with it.

That night, it is impossible to sleep. I am *wired*. I'm on the phone to Nikki until 2.00am, buzzing. Words shooting out of my mouth at record-breaking speed, even for me. When I get to bed my eyes refuse to shut until about 7.00am and then reopen again at 10.00am sharp. I am annihilated. It's an emotional hangover. I get a text from John confirming that, on second thought, given the difficulties to secure the partition screen, counsel agrees it's probably better if I don't go in after all. I roll my eyes under the duvet. *Well, it's a good thing Sarah spotted that one then, isn't it?* It works out well, though, because I am physically incapable of moving from the bed. My arms and legs weigh a tonne. Alison and Erika decide to go in to keep tabs on the case. It's mainly procedural evidence today anyway, so I don't feel too guilty about what they'll be hearing.

That weekend is spent just trying to keep the extreme anxiety at bay. In these types of situations, there's nothing to do but wait, so I try to distract myself and invest in as many small pleasures as possible. Long, searing hot baths with a glass of wine, nice takeaway dinners, cleaning a little to brighten up our space, calls with wholesome friends. Most of the time, I am so physically exhausted I can hardly stand, but I try to find an hour or two each day to get outside and just sit in the sunshine. It's a marathon now, so stamina is key.

* * *

Now that my piece is out of the way, I take in a lot more of what is happening during the second week.

We're back in on Monday morning, and it truly is a circus. Outside the courtroom, we watch the constant procession of comings and goings. Solicitors and barristers balancing toppling towers of papers and binders. A dance of assistants waltzing in with boxes of documents and zooming back out to tell people outside what's happening. Gardaí everywhere, waiting to be called in to give evidence, only to then be thrown back out because the running order of witnesses keeps arbitrarily changing despite having been written down that morning. I catch a glimpse of Bear standing with the other gardaí witnesses (Bear – *swoon*), and they're all clearly frustrated. Looking around the atrium, it seems to be the same for all the other courtrooms, too. Barristers with their black robes billowing around them like something out of Hogwarts, unceremoniously hoisting their gowns back in place as they slide off their shoulders every few minutes. Some of them are lugging around suitcases of paperwork. If you're searching for the culprits of deforestation, look no further than the legal industry. Heaven forbid we move all this to iPads and laptops, that would just defy all reason. A couple of designer handbags aside, you'd swear you were in a Dickens novel. No wonder this is the most inefficient system known to man, we've hardly progressed since the 1800s.

The judge has approved a video-link so that I can watch the proceedings without having to go into the courtroom. Poor John does his best to get the court laptop working, but after forty-five minutes of grappling with the brick of a PC, the link still refuses to work. Erika has been continuing the watching brief in the meantime and gives me the lowdown later. They're on to legal arguments now, and my God it sounds like it's a good thing I wasn't there. Counsel is trying any argument that could worm a small loophole in the law. Defence is arguing that the first sexual assault, which occurred on the bed, terminated the second I woke up and started fighting back, as then the fighting was no longer 'sexual' in nature. Because having a man straddle you in your bed and pin your wrists to your bed with his saliva still wet on your neck isn't sexual, apparently. I'm baffled that such backward arguments can still be voiced out loud in a court of law. Erika gleefully notes that the judge slapped that argument down hard, pointing out that fighting back doesn't stop an assault from being sexual. At least there's still some semblance of common sense in the system.

Erika also explains that there have been a few disruptions from Beast. One of the sergeants told her that he's starting to crack under the pressure. Although he's still not fully alert to what is happening around him and has turned away two translators already, he is getting restless and has started complaining about a pain in his chest. Defence has flagged that he is still refusing to cooperate with them in any way and is highly suspicious of them. He probably cannot differentiate between his team and the State's. I somehow can't help but feel some pity for him. He has so many rules protecting his interests, many to my detriment, like the seizure of my counselling records, he has a team of lawyers working to defend him, and yet he doesn't realise any of it. He probably feels just as alone and uncertain as I do. What a crappy, adversarial system we have got ourselves into.

* * *

The legal arguments continue on Tuesday, and they are *infuriating*. I was warned it might be best not to listen in, and now I see why. The video-link is finally working, so I can witness first-hand the peacocking arrogance of counsel. It's brutal. Watching three men so clinically dissect the most devastating moments of my life and refer to my body parts like they are detached from me is humiliating. I sit through it with gritted teeth. If someone calls me 'the complainant' one more time, I'll actually throw a book at them. I don't know what to do with myself as the rage boils up, so I put my anger to good use and furiously take down notes, word-for-word transcripts of their unending legal arguments, which at this stage feels like a point-scoring competition to me.

Defence counsel, in particular, are vexing. They are trying to artificially fragment the (already short) attack into even shorter segments of time. They are arguing that the assault on the bed amounted to 'just' sexual assault, which then turned into a 'regular' non-sexual assault as the fighting ensued, and that only the last act of penetration amounted to aggravated sexual assault. The reason they're fighting for this is because under law, aggravated sexual assault requires 'serious violence or the threat of serious violence' or causes 'injury, humiliation or degradation'.[11] By artificially dividing the attack into three separate crimes, they're hoping to decouple the element of serious violence, which occurred in the second segment when Beast was strangling me, from the third segment in which the sexual assault occurred.

11 Section 3, Criminal Law (Rape) (Amendment) Act 1990.

In other words, all elements required for aggravated sexual assault were never united in one exact moment in time.

I don't understand how a handful of minutes at most, the most deeply traumatic ones of my life, can be so artificially deconstructed. The angry fireball is in the back of my throat again. Prosecution is strongly countering this and arguing that the aggravated sexual assault happened as a continuum, from the moment Beast got onto the bed to that last violating act. When it is pointed out that fragmenting a few minutes into three separate crimes does not reflect real life, a counterargument is voiced to the effect of, 'But Judge, the *law* does not reflect real life'. And that is why everyone hates lawyers.

Now, I'm all for giving everyone a fair trial, but this is ludicrous. I understand the constitutional importance of Beast's right to fair and due process. I understand it is counsel's job to defend their client and that it's not personal – no problem. But everything must remain within the confines of the law and ethics. *This*, to me, feels like hair-splitting.

The judge rules for Prosecution on the continuum argument but agrees with Defence that were it not for the act of penetration, the entire attack would amount to 'just' sexual assault. A woman who was straddled by a complete stranger who broke into her room at night, who was pinned down to the bed, strangled twice to the point where she thought she would die, with the hand-shaped bruises still decorating her neck a week after the event. That amounts to the same category of offence as being groped on the bus? I will see you all at the gates of hell.

* * *

In the afternoon, we finally move on to closing statements. Counsel for Prosecution finishes his in under fifteen minutes. He is concise and sticks to the facts. He explains how my evidence tallies up perfectly with the medical evidence and forensic photos. He notes how, when the gardaí read my statement to him, Beast initially said that I was telling the truth, then recanted, but could provide no explanation for the 'horrendous' (*heh*) injury on his hand. He also notes that the CCTV footage shows that Beast burgled my apartment, went outside to stash my stuff, and only then came back to commit the sexual assault. Holy SHIT. This is the first I'm hearing of this, and yet that is definite proof of premeditation. Beast isn't some dumb animal who became overcome by lust after all. He knew exactly what he was doing. He showed enough calculating presence of mind to resist his urges long enough to stash his loot and plan his escape after he had raped me.

Counsel for Defence, on the other hand, takes one hour and ten minutes to deliver their closing statement. *Man,* some people love the sound of their own voice. There seems to be no structure or logic to this monologue either. After the first twenty minutes, it again becomes apparent that the sole tactic here is to confuse. The soliloquy is disorganised and muddled, jumping from point to point, but it's not clear what the argument is. They contradict statements, including a couple of points I was crystal clear on. They also make astoundingly brazen statements, like the fact that even though I grabbed Beast by the crotch, *they* were not trying to argue that I sexually assaulted *him*. (The audacity.) Defence gives an example of 'classic sexual' assault as a man in a bar walking past a woman and 'he drops the hand'. They actually say those words out loud in an open courtroom. I glower at them through the computer screen, repeating forgiveness mantras under my breath like Rosary prayers. Needless to say, it does not assuage even an ounce of my loathing right now.

The more Defence talks, however, the more I worry about the jury. Kunak notices I'm tense and points to the screen.

'Look at that juror. And him, him and him. All their arms are crossed. They've already made up their minds, this is just reinforcing that. Defence are digging themselves into a hole right now. The jury hate what they're saying. Look, there goes another one. Arms crossed.'

I nod and try to convince myself that they've made up their minds for the right verdict.

'At this rate, if they don't stop talking, we'll never make it to deliberations today.'

Sure enough, by the time Defence finishes it's 4.00pm and the judge sends everyone home. I fall back into my seat and let out an audible sigh of frustration.

* * *

The next day, it's time for the judge to charge the jury, which means he must summarise the facts of the burglary and the aggravated sexual assault, the evidence and each element of the crimes they must agree happened in order to find Beast guilty. After that, we move to the jury deliberations. *Oh my God, we could have a verdict today.* My heart is bursting through my ribcage.

We arrive early but are told the judge has a juvenile sentencing until 11.30am, so the charging of the jury can only commence at 12.00pm. *That leaves one hour before lunch break, and two hours from 2.00pm to 4.00pm for deliberations. This still could still totally happen today.*

We start with jury instructions at noon, break at 1.00pm for lunch and don't start again until 2.15pm. *We only have four hours each day to get through this CIRCUS and they can't even start on time?* The rage is blazing in my chest again. The judge goes on about the jury having to find Beast guilty 'beyond reasonable doubt' and what exactly that means. He gives so many examples that by the end, even I'm confused.

'This is fucking torture. Can we just get on with it? OH MY GOD, they get what reasonable doubt is. We'll never have time for deliberations now.'

'It's better that he takes as long as possible and is thorough,' explains Margaret. 'If he doesn't take the time now, Defence could try to appeal on the basis that their client didn't get a fair trial.'

'Are you KIDDING ME? They have tried every dirty trick under the sun. This is such a clear-cut case. He's had the fairest trial known to man. It is actually getting ridiculous.'

Margaret gives me a sympathetic smile. 'Trust me on this one, it's for the best.'

The jury finally retire at 3.30pm. The procedural theatrics take ages, between the judge leaving, Beast being taken away, then the jury members retiring four by four. They're called straight back in at 4.00pm – time is up so they'll reconvene tomorrow. I'm tearing my hair out in frustration.

* * *

We walk in just after 11.00am the next day and run into John walking out of the main gates. He's practically bouncing.

'The verdict is back for the first count, the burglary. They found him guilty.'

'Already?!'

'Yeah, they deliberated for all of ten minutes. We're just waiting on the second count now. I have to go speak to my boss, but I'll meet you in the room. I've set up the video-link for you.'

We make our way upstairs and the wait is surreal. We're making small talk as we watch the bustle of the half-empty courtroom on the small screen. Every time I see someone walk in, my heart stops. I can't focus on anything else. The three of us perk up as the courtroom activity picks up noticeably around 11.30am. We see someone approach the law clerk.

'That's the jury minder, isn't it?'

John comes bounding into the room. 'The jury reached a verdict. They're being called back in to deliver it now.'

'That was less than an hour? Is that bad?'

'Impossible to know. We gotta sit tight.'

I swallow. *Here we go.*

Getting everyone back into the courtroom is laborious. Alison, Erika and I are all holding hands, eyes glued to the screen. Whatever I was expecting, it does not come close. It's nothing like what you see in the movies. I thought the foreperson would stand and dramatically deliver the famous words, 'On the count of aggravated sexual assault, we, the jury, find the accused guilty' and theatrical rejoicings in the audience. None of that. Instead, the judge asks the foreperson if they have reached a verdict. The foreperson replies, 'Yes'. The judge asks if the verdict is unanimous. 'Yes.' The judge proceeds to read out the verdict. It's long-winded, summarising what the jury was asked to consider and noting in passing that the jury answered 'Yes' to finding the accused guilty on the first and second count.

'Wait, wait, was that it?'

The judge continues on, and it's hard to hear everything through the video-link.

'Was the second count the aggravated sexual assault?'

'He definitely said guilty, right?'

I don't want to believe it. At this stage I've been shafted too many times by these people and been on so many emotional rollercoasters that my mind tells me it's a trap. *Don't fall for it, Sarah, they're going to change their minds tomorrow because some feckin' procedural detail was missed.* The judge goes on to thank the jury for their service and sets a date in early February for sentencing before dismissing everyone.

And there it was. The most anti-climactic verdict I had ever witnessed. No reaction in the courtroom, no shout from Beast or gasps in the audience, just Alison and Erika clinging on to my hands with tears streaming down their faces. I don't feel anything. The trip switch has been flicked again. I should be hit by a tsunami of emotions, but I got nothing.

'So, that's it?'

I'm watching their faces, wondering why I can't get that same release. This can't be real. I realise in that moment how much they have been through as well. I knew it in my head, but I can see now behind their watery eyes the trauma that they have suffered too. They have hidden it so well to support me, but it's clear the criminal courts have made plenty more than one victim with this case.

After a few minutes John and counsel walk in, beaming. They're talking about how it's such a great outcome and it all came down to my evidence. I hear something about Defence counsel being the 'king of appeals'. I can't take any of it in. As they wrap up and finish talking to Erika and Alison, I mumble something about calling my parents. At this stage, it's almost an excuse to get out of the room. I grab my phone and bolt out the door. I notice I'm running as I make my way towards the ground floor. I need to get outside and feel the air on my face. I'm sprinting now. Past security and through the main gates. Outside, my hands are shaking as I dial the number.

'Sarah? Are you OK?'

'The verdict came back. Guilty on both counts.'

'Oh my God.' Outburst of emotion on the other end of the line.

My knees buckle underneath me and it's all I can do to catch myself on the stone ledge. My mind is back in a state of dissociation. Everything feels fuzzy again. My face can't stop smiling, but my body is having a complete meltdown. The physical waves of release of months of built-up tension are rocketing through my body. A couple of tears eventually make it to my eyes.

The nightmare is over.

SURVIVAL GUIDE: THE TRIAL

As you'll have seen by now, even with the strongest and most clear-cut evidence, there are a lot areas you can get tripped up in. I wanted to open the court doors and let everyone see the shocking things that unfold behind them. These are our courts, our justice system, they are there to serve us, not to act as a playground for the legal profession to make it so extraordinarily complicated for us, the people, to obtain justice. So now, I want to recap on the elements you need to arm yourself with going into that war zone.

Decide if you want to bring people with you when giving your evidence: this is your decision, but you should know that it could destabilise you to see their reactions. You will be asked very intrusive and sometimes painful questions. They will also be asked to leave if they have any audible or visible reaction that could influence the jury (even something as small as raising eyebrows). If your family or friends do attend, brief them to not show any reaction whatsoever. There is no exact number of people you are allowed to bring with you. It is usually around three or four, but could be fewer, particularly if the accused (who is also allowed to have family or a support person present) has no one in the room. It might be easier to bring someone more removed, like an accompanier from the Dublin Rape Crisis Centre (www.drcc.ie/services/accompaniment/).

The most important people in the room are you and the jury: look at them when you're speaking, make eye contact. You can look at the barristers when they ask you a question, but then ignore them and look at the jury when you are answering. They are the people you need to convey the information to, no one else. Paint the picture for them, watch their body language and adjust your tone if you need to.

No matter what happens, stay calm and respectful: that will help your credibility and get the jury on your side. Defence may try to upset you or ask difficult questions, but if you get defensive or aggressive that will only turn the jury against you. Remember the jury are human, too. They will respect you for rising above. If Defence ask you a difficult question (e.g. 'were you drinking?'), answer it factually and move on. There will always be questions you don't like, but do not get defensive. It will not help your case.

Don't get thrown by the formalities: once Prosecution are done, Defence will cross-examine you. This is a formal process in which they will "put" their arguments to you (e.g. "I put it to you that you were mistaken about the time this happened"). This just means they are suggesting to you that their argument is true. You should respond to these questions with "Yes" or "No" (and, if "No", explain why you disagree to the jury). One Defence tactic to be aware of is that they will put a number of undisputed facts to you, to get you to agree with them several times and lull you into a false sense of security, before placing an argument in favour of their client. Answer each question as it comes, do not be influenced by the one that came before it.

Be aware of Defence's behaviour: if the barrister gets aggressive towards you or has disrespectful body language (e.g. putting their foot up on the bench, readjusting or tugging at the waistline of their trousers, raising their voice or even making distracting noises while you are speaking like constantly rustling papers or loudly sighing), <u>do not react</u>. It is intended to destabilise you, so don't give them what they want. The less you react, the more they will look stupid to the jury.

Stand up for yourself and call it out: you may expect Prosecution to object, but they may not. If Defence's behaviour gets out of hand, call it out (respectfully). This is the nuke button, <u>so don't overplay it</u>. You can say (very calmly): 'I'm sorry, I am a sexual assault victim. I am understandably still very traumatised and I find your body language quite triggering. Could you please stop [putting your foot on the bench]?'

It's totally normal to feel vulnerable or emotional: everyone understands how hard this is for you. If you do cry or get shaky, don't worry. I know how vulnerable you feel, but remember that can only help your credibility, not hurt it. You can ask for a break at any time if it gets too overwhelming, just to walk outside and take a breath (sometimes the judge might even suggest this for you).

Convey, don't convince: an obvious one, but stick to the truth. You are most believable when you are yourself. There is no better defence than the truth. That said, a trial is most definitely theatre (with costumes and everything). It is a display for the benefit of the judge and jury, and counsel know that. So you want to convey the information, not convince the jury of it. Try to project your voice enough, make eye contact with the jury and pause when you need to, to let your words sink in.

Never guess the answer to a question: if you do not know or are not sure, say so. For example, you can say, 'I know it was after 2.00am because I went to bed at 1.00am, but I do not know the exact time'. Do not give Defence any opportunity to challenge your credibility.

Do not let anyone put words in your mouth: Defence will often try to make you say something in their favour (e.g. 'I put it to you that you liked the accused making advances to you'). Do not be afraid to say, 'I never said that' or 'That is not correct', and then correct their statement. This will also make you sound clear and rational to the jury.

Watch out when it comes to intention: if Defence tries to get you to comment on someone's (particularly the accused's) intention or state of mind, point out that you cannot possibly speak to that. However, if the answer could work in your favour, e.g. 'Did the accused think you consented?', you can point out the relevant circumstances, e.g. 'I can't speak to his state of mind, but I was clearly passed out and so, incapable of consenting' or 'I screamed and resisted, so any reasonable person would not believe I was consenting'.

Speak slowly: pause after the question is put to you and don't be afraid to take your time in answering. This will not only give you time to think through your answer, it also gives you poise and dignity and that will make you feel more confident. You've waited long enough to be here, this is your time to tell your story. Take your time and tell it in full.

If you don't understand a question, you can ask for it to be repeated or clarified: this can also give you time to think if you're destabilised by the question.

If a question seems odd to you, ask the judge for guidance: for example, if you're worried about mentioning something that you feel would compromise the case in any way, you can turn to the judge and say, 'I'm not sure how to answer that without mentioning something that may not be directly related to this case, Judge'.

Bring a few tissues: tissues and water will usually be provided, but no harm in having some handy, and personally I found it was comforting to have something to hold on to.

Remember you will always feel like you left something out: everyone feels that way. Do not beat yourself up about it. This is one of the hardest things you'll ever have to do and you did your best. If it's really important, write it down in the notes as part of your preparation. (But remember, you cannot take these notes in with you.)

Do not talk about the accused's character or past sexual history, only what happened to you: this is <u>ABSOLUTELY CRITICAL</u> as it could lead to a mistrial, because it affects the accused's right to presumption of innocence until proven guilty. This has tanked trials before. I know it's not fair that they can get a character witness and you can't, that they can in certain circumstances go snooping into your sexual history and not the accused's, but the last thing you want is to see the accused walk because of something you said. A tragic recent example of this I was given by someone: a man had raped two women but went on separate trials for each crime. When giving her evidence, the first victim referred to the second. The whole trial collapsed as a result.

If you are interrupted but you were not done speaking, tell them (respectfully): this is *your* time to tell your story, so let no one bully you. Unfortunately, no one will stand up for you, so you have to be prepared to do it for yourself (but stay very respectful, you don't want to come across as defensive). You can say things like, 'I'm sorry, but I wasn't done and this is important' or 'This is understandably very distressing for me, so could you please not rush me?'

Do not be afraid to (respectfully) contest things: just because you are dealing with figures of authority does not mean they are gods. The black robes and wigs are a smokescreen. The judges and barristers are humans, just like you and me. And humans make mistakes. You are entitled to query and contest things (again, respectfully – we catch more flies with honey than with vinegar). And always put everything in writing if it happens in the lead up to your testifying or relates to something procedural, like the partition screen.

After it's over, let it go: you did your absolute best. Whatever happens afterwards, it's out of your hands and does not reflect badly on you in any way. You have nothing to regret and should feel extremely proud of yourself. Regardless of the outcome, know that you <u>can</u> and <u>will</u> heal and move on from this, too.

You are not abandoned after the trial: accompaniment services like those offered by the Rape Crisis Centre will not stop once the trial ends. Your accompanier will continue checking in with you afterwards and at particular milestones, such as sentencing. You can also continue to receive therapy and other supports. You are not alone here.

Remember that in Ireland there is a 25% remission of sentences: if there is a guilty verdict, whatever sentence is imposed will automatically be reduced by a quarter, meaning if a ten-year prison sentence is imposed, only 7.5 years will actually be served; if a five-year sentence is imposed, only four will be served, etc. Insane, I know. That was a huge shock for me to find out months after the verdict, so better to know in advance and be ready for it.

Look into restorative justice: if a court case is not open to you, or if you do not get the verdict you hoped for, there are alternatives that may be more effective, like restorative justice between the perpetrator and yourself. There are lots of materials online to give you a sense of whether this would be appropriate for you.

9.

Claim your Baggage: The Question of Anonymity

Diary entry, 6 March 2021
'We did it.'

After the trial was over, all I wanted to do was to put the whole experience in a box, bury it deep in the ground and never speak of it again. For weeks afterwards, Alison and I were in a daze. It was only in writing this book and talking things over with her that we came to realise how we never properly debriefed after it was all over. Even two years later. True to our Irish roots, when the subject came up, we brandished humour as a shield to deflect the trauma we were put through. Questions would be shrugged off with a weak grin and, 'It was pretty crap alright' or '*Yeah*, let's never do that again'. We were so burnt by the entire process that all we could do was crawl away and sweep the whole thing under a rug until it shrivelled down to a nasty, distant memory.

We were marooned survivors on a desert island. Having just about managed to miraculously survive the violent storm that had sunk our ship and dragged our heavy bodies ashore, we had little energy left to do much else than just recover. There was everything we needed here, food, water, shelter, warmth and, above all else, lack of anguish. The ancient Greeks had a word for this place – ataraxia. The word literally translates to 'lack of disturbance' or 'absence of trouble'. It refers to an idyllic state of complete peace and serenity, free from all pain and anxiety. It is one level up from aponia, which is the lack of physical pain. You know that sensation when you have a torturous toothache or sciatica for days and one day you wake up and it's just gone? That sweet, blissful-bordering-on-orgasmic release is aponia. Ataraxia is the absence of both physical and mental troubles.

I was content, but not fulfilled. Don't get me wrong, it was comfortable, this place of total tranquillity, undisturbed by the bullshit of court or the fiery demons of anger. That wiry ball trapped at the back of my throat and in the pit of my stomach had just vanished. I could have stayed there forever. In fact, I probably would have, if something hadn't dislodged me from there. That thing came in February, nearly two months after the verdict was handed down.

Sentencing was delayed by a month, *quelle surprise*, but another hearing was set in February for my Victim Impact Statement. In Ireland, if you are a victim (**cough** witness) of a crime, you can, after a guilty verdict, give an account of the impact that crime has had on you. Its purpose is to help the judge understand all consequences of the crime before setting the sentence. The *real* purpose, however, is to make you feel heard. There is no number of years the judge could announce that would bring you peace. But the opportunity to speak out about the ordeal you endured, after having been silenced and prevented from speaking about your story due to court rules for so long, is an important psychological step in finding your closure.

Victim Impact Statements were fought for hard by hero Lavinia Kerwick, the first rape survivor to waive anonymity in Ireland. Lavinia was raped on New Year's Eve 1991, and she campaigned fearlessly for reforms to the oppressive justice system that allowed her rapist to walk free with a suspended sentence. Writing an impact statement is not mandatory. It is entirely your decision. But it is the chance to hand some of the guilt and weight you've been carrying with you back to your abuser and the court. They must all listen in silence as you (or someone you nominate) reads it out and there are no rebuttals, questions or counterarguments allowed.

One of the most important things to know about it is how little notice you are given to write it. For a system that loves to delay and take its sweet time, I was given four weeks to send in my statement, despite having begged for details of what to include in it for over a year. What saved me was my diaries. You start writing this statement in your head well before proceedings ever begin, but it is crucial to prepare the groundwork by keeping detailed records of every impact, every setback, every change to your life. Each time I got into a fight with my family about being touched or found myself getting panicky at parties, I would whip out my phone and make a note of the incident to transcribe into the journal later. That little Horcrux diary that I had acquired was quickly joined by two more as I ran out of pages to unload my eighteen-month emotional cascade onto. Forgive the solicitor getting excited here, but that is the beauty of contemporaneous notes. I could not get over how much I had blurred from my memory. I remembered the PTSD and the anger, sure, but the details and volume at which it appeared throughout these diaries was astounding.

Now, I won't lie to you, putting it all down on paper is excruciating. It was a world of pain, not only re-reading all of my notes but then condensing two years of my life ruled by extreme PTSD and the torture of the trial down into a five-page statement. It took me a full month to write it. I found myself staring at my computer screen for hours on end, forced to relive every detail because I wanted to capture the full impact of those eighteen months. Not because I wanted to influence the sentence, but for my own closure.

In terms of logistics, the statement must be in your own words, but there is no right or wrong format for it. Never something a lawyer wants to hear. Like any respectable commercial solicitor, I was adamant on finding a precedent to understand what exactly was expected. Needless to say, I found none. I plagued John with questions – how many pages for this yoke? Is there a maximum length? Is there an expected style or standard? How much detail do I go into? The answer was always the same – there are no specifications, just say it in your own words. From speaking with different gardaí, my understanding is that they are on average at least three to four pages (about 2,000 words).

There are four headings to fill out:

Economic loss: this is any property lost or damaged as a result of the crime, and any medical or hospital bills you had to cover. Receipts are ideal, if you have them, but they're not required. And it's not like you get any of that money back anyway, so don't worry too much about those.

Physical injuries: this one speaks for itself, but it also includes any medical treatment like Pre-exposure prophylaxis (PrEP), the morning-after pill, hepatitis B shots, and so on. It also very much covers any of their side-effects (nausea, pain, dizziness, hormonal changes, etc.), as you would not have been subjected to that medication were it not for the crime.

Psychological / Psychiatric effects and/or treatment needed: this was a long one. I broke mine into chronological sub-sections: (a) the immediate aftermath of the crime (the shock and panic in SATU); (b) the intermediate aftermath (basically all of Chapter 4 – PTSD; panic attacks, insomnia, flashbacks, nightmares, aversion to touch); (c) the extreme stress and anxiety in the lead-up to the trial; and (d) my ongoing counselling and therapy.

Life / Long-term changes: these are all of the changes in your personal or family life. You can cover any impacts on your family or loved ones. I would strongly advise including the trauma they have been put through as well, resulting not only from the crime but also from the trial.

Not sure what to include? If in doubt, cover everything. Anything connected to the crime, even indirectly, is relevant. You want to paint a very clear picture, not just of what you endured during the assault and trial, but also the long-term impacts that followed. Be as honest and complete as possible – you don't want to look back and regret not having done yourself justice. This is *your* chance to speak about what you have been through. If you decide not to go public, this may be one of the only moments you will have to feel seen by people outside of your circle, so seize it.

The reading of the statement in court is empowering because you are the one giving yourself closure. No one else will do it for you. You have had to sit through all that bullshit and listen to those peacocks puff their chests and ramble on about your genitals in court for weeks, so now you take your time and let them have it. Get it off your chest and into those goddamn people's ears.

Now, I'm a sucker for templates, so to give you a sense of the scope, I have pulled extracts from my statement as an example. I'm only pulling from headings 3 and 4, as the first two are much less detailed and more straightforward.

III. PSYCHOLOGICAL / PSYCHIATRIC EFFECTS AND TREATMENT:

In the hours immediately following the crime, I was in shock. I felt completely numb, unable to feel any emotion as I recounted the facts to the police and doctors, only dull nausea and extreme apathy. I was in a state of dissociation where everything felt surreal and nothing mattered anymore.

This state of shock and panic worsened over several months. I could not bear to be touched by anyone, not even my own parents, which was agonising as we are a very close and affectionate family. The sensation, even the mere thought, of someone touching me made my skin crawl and triggered extreme panic attacks, which translated into physical symptoms such as hyperventilation, a pounding heart, uncontrollable crying and shaking. I was frightened of being near people in case they tried to hug or touch me.

I was in a state of extreme hypervigilance for months. All my senses were on high alert, despite being constantly exhausted. I compulsively checked that the windows and doors of the room I was in were locked up to 20–30 times at night. I lived in constant fear that I would be attacked and violated in my sleep again.

Certain sensory reminders would spark a state of panic in me. The sound of running made me freeze. Things that were previously so ordinary, like walking down a mildly crowded street, suddenly were a nightmare. Wherever possible, I would have to stand with my back to the wall.

IV. LIFE CHANGES:

To this day I do not feel safe. The fact that I was so violently attacked in the safe haven that was my bed, in the privacy of my bedroom, means that there is nowhere that feels safe to me, not even the sanctity of my own home. I am frightened of falling asleep. My body resists any form of unconsciousness because I do not feel safe. I no longer know what it is to wake peacefully.

For everyone else life has moved on, but for me time has stopped. I watch as my friends and family look to the future and don't think about the crime anymore, but I feel I do not have a future to look forward to. I am stuck, unable to move past that night of the crime when my life was turned upside down. It never leaves me. It is the first thing I think of in the morning and the last thing I think of at night. I carry it with me every day, it is a weight that sometimes crushes my chest, invisible to the rest of the world but very real to me.

The trial was one of the worst experiences of my life. I have never felt so vulnerable or humiliated. I am deeply hurt by it and think about it often. Not being allowed to speak freely about being a sexual violence victim was a huge barrier to my recovery. For nearly two years, I have felt silenced about something that was not my fault, when all I wanted was to tell the world so that people would know what I was going through and I wouldn't feel so alone. The violation and violence I was subjected to I felt on such a deep psychological level that I believe it has become a core part of who I am.

I am fighting hard to heal, body and mind, from the horror and ordeal that has been these past 18 months. I do not want to look back to what has happened in anger or regret, but I know that the life I had before the crime is gone, and I am still grieving for that life. I am heartbroken for my family, heartbroken over the many losses this crime has cost me, and heartbroken that no one will ever fully understand what I went through, what I still go through every day. This crime, which only lasted a number of minutes, has left an irreparable mark on my life and the life of my family that will never fully go away.

That gives you some idea of how to approach your Statement. Remember, though, yours must be in your own words. Write from the heart and you cannot go wrong.

* * *

I delivered my Victim Impact Statement by video-link, as I was still too fragile after the trial to leave my family. I couldn't stop my voice from breaking or the tears from streaming down my face as I read out my five pages. Halfway through my reading, counsel for Defence got up and walked out. After everything I had been put through, the humiliation I had to stomach throughout the trial, it was a slap in the face. There may have been a very good reason for this exit, nonetheless it astounds me that this was allowed to happen. This is the only time the victim is allowed to speak to the trauma they have endured and how their life has changed. It is a basic courtesy that they be afforded the respect of being listened to for those twenty minutes without interruption. If you need to leave, you either go before it begins, or you wait until she or he is done. In my eyes, nothing could summarise better the lack of feckin' respect our justice system affords survivors.

Another fiasco happened that day, however, that inched me closer to my decision to go public. At the start of the hearing my video-link was tested for sound and image quality. The criminal court's panelled walls are dotted with large TV monitors, and the judge, clerks and counsel each have separate, smaller monitors on their desks. What should have happened is that my video should have come up on the individual monitors only, so that Beast could not see me. Instead, there was a heart-dropping moment when my face popped up on all the TVs, not just the judge's and counsels', and displayed very clearly on my own laptop was the full courtroom, with Beast in clear view. I froze. This was my first time seeing him cold, and nothing could have prepared me for it. There was absolutely no partition there to screen me off from his line of sight either.

After all that work, after all those Vulnerability Assessments and hearings and months of jumping through all those hoops to get the partition screen to protect my safety, Beast could see me. And I saw him. Prosecution quickly realised the error and pulled the link, but it was too late. With shaking hands I texted Erika and Kunak, who were both sitting in the courtroom.

'Did he see me?'

'I'm not sure. You were only up on the TVs for a minute. Hopefully he didn't register who you were.'

Failed by the justice system. Again. The larger monitors could not be disconnected, so there was a scramble to locate the partition screen again. It became painfully apparent that everyone had forgotten about it. The search party delayed the hearing for another thirty minutes. I heard someone in the courtroom sigh 'this is a disaster' and I saw red. This was *your* responsibility, I hissed internally. When I'm giving a presentation in work, I make sure my laptop and slides are lined up the night before. I fail to understand how people can be so exasperatingly inefficient and unprepared, particularly in an industry that administers national justice.

On 1 March 2021, the sentencing hearing was held. After my Victim Impact Statement and the presenting of mitigating factors by Defence, the judge sentenced Beast to ten years in prison. As he read out the sentence, I received it with very mixed emotions. Happiness certainly wasn't one of them. It was remarked to me that even life imprisonment would not be enough for what Beast had done, and yet I couldn't help but feel a pang of pity for him. Someone like that has never had a chance in life. As much as he should be kept away from society, what he really needs is serious rehabilitation if he is ever going to change. Rotting in jail for a decade is just going to turn him into even more of an outcast.

* * *

My instinct had been telling me to speak out for a long time. Even in those first few weeks after the attack, when I worked so hard to hide what had really happened. Even when a legal professional told me to say nothing in my law firm because it would brand me as fragile and I would be passed over for work, which would ruin my career. Even then, something deep down inside me knew I would speak out about this one day. I was just biding my time.

I had asked the DPP about it in the summer of 2020, when organising a Busy Warrior Yoga fundraiser for the Rape Crisis Centre, which was in desperate need of funds during the COVID-19 pandemic. When I asked if I could say that I was a sexual violence victim at this event, assuring them there would be no disclosure of any evidence or even mention of a trial, I was met with a response as cold as it was dispiriting: *'Pre-trial, the complainant should not be raising money for charity by discussing directly or indirectly, generally or specifically the fact that she has been a victim of sexual violence. This is because legally, there has been no finding of guilt.'*

Frosty. Also, technically inaccurate. Legally speaking, no finding of guilt does not mean no crime has been committed, only that no one has been found responsible for that crime. The sexual violence happened, that is a matter of fact.

As the horrors of the criminal justice process continued to unfold in the year that followed, it only served to fuel my call to arms. But what ultimately crystallised my decision to go public was the media coverage of the case. As sentencing had not yet taken place, I was advised to stay silent until then, to not jeopardise the case. I had been assured numerous times that nothing would be published in the media until the sentencing. *Wrong.*

The day of the Victim Impact Statement hearing, a number of appalling news articles started popping up in various Irish tabloids and newspapers. They were pure shock value, stripped of all empathy and clearly written with the sole intent of making money on the back of this sensationalised story. There was zero thought for how this would read to the traumatised victim, or her family. Salt concentrations – one hundred percent. It was such a shock, not only because the articles came with no warning and were not supposed to appear until sentencing, but also because, despite not being named, I was unmistakably identifiable from the facts, some of which were inaccurately or exaggeratedly reported. Ireland is a small country – a story as heart-stopping as a burglar attempting to rape and murder a woman in her sleep does the rounds very quickly. And now, thanks to these incredibly insensitive articles, everyone knew the full extent of the gruesome, intimate details of my violation.

Sure enough, floods of texts and messages started pouring in from a wide range of people, some of whom I had not spoken to in years. I felt fury and devastation, again. After enduring the ordeal of the criminal justice process, I was not even allowed to come out on my own terms. The salt-bearing, dirt-digging press had stolen my story from me without even bothering to consult me or ask for my views.

The articles also named Beast, which was the one thing I did not want. This was my story, but they made it about him. I knew people would latch on to his nationality and make it about that and not about the issue at hand – namely, sexual violence and how we treat survivors. Sure enough, the aggressive racism in the Comments section triggered by his name made me sick to my stomach. Some commentators were almost gleefully conjecturing whether my views on asylum-seekers had changed after being violated. As if no white man had ever committed such a heinous crime. They dared to piggy-back on my trauma to further their hate speech and racist political agenda, when actually sexual violence has no race, creed or colour. I think I understand better than most what it is to feel unsafe. People are coming to our shores fleeing crimes far more terrifying than the one I survived. There is no difference between those people and me, except the luck of the draw of where we were born.

The media plays a huge role in how we treat sexual violence survivors as a society. I am all for free press, but with that freedom and influence comes responsibility. As we move worldwide towards a more sustainable economy, not just environmentally but socially too, it is up to the key stakeholders to take on their share of accountability. It is not sustainable for survivors for the media to report on sexual violence and sexual assault in a way that deters them from coming forward and embracing their healing journey. It is no longer acceptable to feed into toxic culture that normalises rape and views it as women's problem. How many times have you read headlines to the effect of 'woman raped' or 'teenage girl abused' – as if rape is something that just *happens* as you're about your day. The sole cause of the rape, the rapist, is not even acknowledged in that sentence. Rape and sexual assault are everyone's problem. It is as much about how we raise our sons as we do our daughters.

There are already plenty of ethical guidelines and codes of conduct regulating the media industry, and these should always be living documents. Now that we have the resources to inform ourselves on the harmful impacts of sensationalist headlines and reporting, there are no more excuses not to embed that responsibility in those guidelines. We all have a duty, individually, to educate ourselves, but with the power the media holds, they should be using their influence to at least balance out articles by raising awareness on sexual assault, not contributing to survivors' trauma. And we, the people, need to hold the media to account by speaking out against such practices.

Those articles were the straw that broke the camel's back. I had nothing left to lose now. Beast knew my face, and now my darkest secret was exposed for all to see. So I decided to claim my baggage and set the record straight in the process. If my insights could help even one other person, it would be worth it. For so long I had stayed in the shadows, finally it was time to step into the light.

I reached out to journalist and champion of women, Una Mullally. Erika set up the introduction and from my very first contact with her, my healing began. In stark contrast to the intrusive news articles, she was sensitive, invested in the long-term learnings of my story for society at large, level-headed, and demonstrated the utmost professionalism. She asked the right questions and gave weight to the right elements. She was fearless in the face of my trauma and gentle in her advice to carve out time after every meeting to recuperate. She just let me talk. It took us three interviews, of several hours each, to draw out the full story. After being silenced for so long, all I could do was word-vomit at her. That process, I later understood, would seal my final narrative on my story and allow me to claim it in its entirety.

We waited until after sentencing to publish the article. It was the most daunting thing I have ever done in my life, and I don't regret it one iota. It was liberating. I was finally free to speak and leave all this behind me. We debated on including certain parts of the story, but after the devastation of being so blind-sided by the earlier articles, I never wanted to feel that way again. We agreed to release everything. No one would ever be able to hurt me like that again by exposing some new detail to spew their shock value, because I had already put it all out there. I put my name and face to it, too, because I wanted to practice what I preach and show there is nothing to be ashamed of, that there is no reason we should have to hide or suffer in silence.

The story broke on the morning of Saturday, 6 March 2021. I don't know what I was expecting, but nothing could have prepared me for the tidal wave of support, the words of encouragement, and most of all the dozens and dozens of women and men who shared their own stories with me. As painful as the trial was, going public was where I finally found my closure. The trauma, the rage, the heartbreak and anguish of the past two years, it all disappeared with the kindness, connections and emotion that flooded towards me that day. Love really does conquer all.

Una's beautifully crafted article struck a nerve. The public response to it shone a light on the all-too-common pattern we have been seeing recently of survivors silenced and humiliated and traumatised, all in the name of justice. And after every such case, always the same outcry – how many more stories like these is it going to take for our justice system to change?

The domino effect from Una's article, from radio coverage to the social media reaction, led to meetings with the DPP and the Minister for Justice. They were encouragingly receptive, but we all know how slow institutions are to enact reform. We need to seize this moment and keep the pressure on because the time for change is now. With enough support, I whole-heartedly believe we can achieve this change. You, me, all of us.

* * *

There are some things to know if you do decide the path of public disclosure is for you. The first is that in the era of the internet, once you go public, you have crossed the Rubicon. There is no going back. So you need to take your time with this decision. The second is that no matter who you are or what happened to you, there are going to be haters. Even queen Beyoncé has them. The online world is a breeding ground for haters and trolls, who often hide behind secondary accounts. As infuriating as they may be, do not engage. Do not let those salt-bearers contaminate the oasis you have built from the ashes up. Clear the salt by blocking, ignoring, or killing with kindness. They are bored individuals looking for a reaction, they should be pitied not hated. And while we're on the subject, if you fall into this category, would you do me a favour and grab a pen and paper and list ten nice things about yourself. Go on, try it, it might honestly curtail the need to write nasty things about other people for a little while. I'm sending some healing love your way.

I speak extremely personally in this chapter. Waiving your anonymity may not be for you. You may be at peace without going down that route, you may not wish to revisit that part of your life. My reaching out to Una was a personal choice. It was based in no small degree on the fact that I did not have to deal with seeing Beast's family, his friends, locals at the pub or randomers on the street who know of him. Your situation may be very different. This is your decision alone to make. There is no right or wrong when it comes to something as important as this.

The only right is your truth, and you don't have to go to the newspapers to speak it. You may feel you cannot go public about your story, even if you want to. Your abuser may have walked free because our justice system failed you, and that is the greatest injustice of them all. You may be waiting for a trial and feel silenced until then. But you still have a choice. And there are many ways of speaking your truth that do not involve going public. You can say a lot without naming the abuser or going into detail about what happened. The abuser is almost irrelevant here – this is about you, your resilience, your trauma, your healing. You can embody your truth every day, by embracing each aspect of your journey that has brought you here and set you on your trajectory to become a stronger, deeper, more compassionate soul.

Talking about rape and sexual assault takes us far outside of our comfort zone, but it is outside that zone that we truly connect with others and ourselves. If your truth scares people away, and it will, those people were never meant to be in your life. They were salt-bearers to you. People will only ever be able to connect with you at the level they are at. Some will never outgrow a certain threshold, and they will be unable to meet you past that point. That has nothing to do with you.

At whatever level you do speak your truth, the point is not to hide from your own story. Secrets are poison. That's not a figure of speech. Exactly like holding on to anger, it is literally toxic to conceal negative secrets. You are wasting valuable energy holding onto such things that are weighing you down, and over time they become a breeding ground for shame, guilt, stress and loneliness. Bottling them up or avoiding them is another form of salt, and it will catch up with you. To clear the salt, you must draw them into the open. Even if you tell no one else – although I very much hope that, in time, you do tell someone – the most important person to tell your story to is yourself.

You are the author of your own story. You, and only you, control its parameters. Some people may call you a victim, a survivor, a complainant. What matters is the language you choose. Words matter, yes, but the most important words are those you decide on, and the people you honour by sharing them with. Even if your story has been put out into the world, even if it was not on your own terms, the world has not heard *your* story, and yours is the only one of importance. Whether you put it down on paper for yourself, speak it to only one friend or to a counsellor or post about it online, you cannot go too far wrong with your truth.

SURVIVAL GUIDE: THE QUESTION OF ANONYMITY

I'm going to sound like a broken record, but again, this is such a personal decision. Only you can make it, but there are some crucial things you should know and consider before making it.

Remember, there is no formal procedure to waive your anonymity: for all the courts talk about 'waiving anonymity', there is no one way for you to do it. Take your time to decide on what platform or media you want to go public, and the possibilities for people to comment on or share your story.

Be prepared for media coverage after the verdict: you should know that, regardless of what you want, your case may be reported in the news. You will not be named, but the offender will be (unless this could identify you, e.g. if it was a family member). The court reporters are present throughout the case and when you read out your Victim Impact Statement, so they can report on any parts of it, without consulting you. You should also prepare yourself for it not being in the papers at all. If it's a busy day for the news, the story may not feature. Be ready either way.

Take your time with this decision because once it's online, you cannot take it back: there is no backtracking once it's hit the internet. I knew early on that this was what I wanted to do and there were times when I felt frustrated that I couldn't speak out sooner, but looking back I don't regret having had to wait nearly two years because by then I was certain of my decision and ready for whatever the consequences might be.

Never go public reactively: if you see something online or read an article about your case, resist the urge to waive your anonymity in the moment. You may think you need to go public then or the moment will pass, but for the same reason as above, you want this to be *your* decision, not a decision someone caused you to make. I'm not telling you to ignore your instinct, but I am suggesting that you sleep on it, for a little while. This decision could change your life. If it's the right one, you'll feel the same way in a few weeks' time.

Consider any impacts on your family and friends: it's completely understandable to think about how this decision will affect you, but be aware that it may change the lives of your loved ones too. That in itself should never be a reason to stop you from speaking your truth, but you might want to consider discussing it with them beforehand. Also think about if there is anything they need to do beforehand, like putting their social media on private or talking to a therapist.

Think of the reasons why you want to do it: are you going public out of revenge or spite, to embrace your story, or to raise awareness about sexual assault? Be sure your reasons are the right ones (and only you can know that).

Pick your moment: line up your counselling sessions, and do it at a time when you feel strong and ready. You alone are in control of the timing of your story being released.

If there is any chance of this still going to court, consider waiting: once you go public, even if you only talk about you and keep it very general, there is a chance that at trial stage Defence will argue that the accused is not getting a fair trial and this could collapse the proceedings. If this is a risk you're not willing to live with, then it's worth waiting – in spite of your disappointment and frustration. I know it's not fair, but you owe it to your future self if there's even a chance of a trial.

Understand that once you go public, you no longer control the narrative of your story: this is particularly important if you are releasing only part of the story. People may link you to other articles written about the case and anyone, including the convict and their family, will be free to speak too. Think long and hard about any aspects that could be released by someone else once you've waived your anonymity. Even if you put it out on your own terms, once it's online you cannot control how people will manipulate, reshare, comment or report on it.

If you're not 100% certain about going public, I would advise against it: better to wait a while and be sure than do it impulsively and regret it later. You're in control of the timing, and it is never too late to do it.

Remember that posting online includes waiving your anonymity, it is not limited to newspapers or TV: once you have put your name to the story, your anonymity is gone and people (including the perpetrator or their family) will be free to write or talk about the case, so talk it through with a few friends or family members. They might help you to identify things you hadn't considered. This will not only help you to reach your decision but also to be prepared for anything once you do.

Do a full social media check beforehand: people will look you up and may try to contact you. Check the privacy settings are exactly what you want across all your accounts. Check your personal details aren't on any platforms (including old blogs and random websites you may have previously done work with). Google your name to see if your home address or phone number come up anywhere.

Think of what you legally cannot say: if there was no guilty verdict or admission of guilt, you likely cannot name the perpetrator. Even with a guilty verdict, there will be things you cannot say. God knows, there are still things I can't speak about. But that does not stop you from speaking about your experience as a sexual assault survivor or talking about the person that matters the most here, *you*.

No matter who you are or what happened to you, there will be haters: some people are bored and angry and have nothing better to do than try to get a reaction out of you. Regardless of their motives, do not engage. You are holy, and you will not sacrifice your integrity by engaging in a tit-for-tat with people who are set on taking you down with them.

Get legal advice if you're concerned about anything: even just to be clear on what you can and cannot say, or what the consequences of certain aspects may be. It will bring you peace of mind and will be one less thing to worry about. Remember, you are entitled to free legal aid for certain types of sexual offence (more on this in the Survival Guide for Chapter 7).

10.

Ash + Salt: Healing

Diary entry, 3 November 2019:
'This is my strength, not my weakness. I can do anything.'

Healing is a process. It takes practice, it takes patience, it takes time. It is a choice you make every day to let the wound be the place where the light enters you. You have to choose to let go, again and again, until one day you are free.

After an ordeal like yours, you may believe that you cannot come back from this. The unthinkable has happened. The volcanic eruption of trauma that has shaken you to your roots has passed, leaving nothing but a field of ashes in its wake. Around you, there are cinders as far as the eye can see. And yet, this is where you will set the scene for your healing. This is the place from which you will rise and keep on ascending. The ash is your blank canvas, and *you* decide what aspects of your previous life you wish to replant and what you let go of. In time, the seeds you have planted will blossom and flourish more beautifully than the life that grew before it ever could. But before you sow them, you must clear away the salt. The toxic element that prevents new life from taking root and thriving.

Some forms of salt we have control over, starting with the first layer – bad sleep, poor diet or not getting enough exercise. A healthy mind starts with a healthy body, that is your starting point. You cannot heal in a toxic environment, so it is crucial to start seriously investing your time and energy in your physical well-being. Your number one priority must become your rest, going out for walks, jogs or swims, getting that sunshine and vitamin D on your skin and some wholesome food into your body.

The second layer of salt is a little trickier but is still internal. In this layer, we have less tangible things, like holding on to negative thoughts, being unkind to ourselves, or refusing to recognise our grief. These are still within our control and there is a lot we can do to get a handle on them, starting by acknowledging those thoughts, allowing ourselves to be present with them, and ultimately reframing them though therapy or mindfulness. Tackling this layer takes longer, and for me it required professional help. As strong as you are, this is something too great for anyone to take on fully by themselves. (More on dealing with negative emotions at Chapter 5.)

The third layer of salt stems from things outside of our control – toxic environments, toxic jobs and toxic people. As these things are external to us, we may feel we have no control over them, but actually there is a lot we can do about them. We always have a choice, to surround ourselves with positivity and let go as much toxicity as possible.

Personally, I found this third layer especially difficult. In particular, I struggled to deal with toxic people and friends – the 'salt-bearers', as I came to call them. There are salt-bearers everywhere in your life – the moaners and groaners, the perpetual criticisers, passive-aggressive people, judgemental people, people who are negative about everything, narcissists, liars, people who do not respect your boundaries, 'friends' who always take from you but never seem to give back.

In the months that followed the attack and those that led up to the trial, many people from my circle let me down badly. From friends who had always been there in the good times to those who had supported me professionally, they wanted nothing to do with this now. They left me behind, and it slowly gnawed a hole into my heart. I was forgotten, and the pain was only greater because some of these people were from my closest circles. I had been there for them time after time. I was there to celebrate the small wins, stood by them through the break-ups, the failures, the anxiety, the deaths, the family fights and the rough patches. I had turned up with flowers and cake in the good times, hugs and vodka in the bad. And yet now, in my greatest time of need, so few had shown up. That's one of the unexpected side-effects of a trauma like this: it throws into light where the genuine relationships stand in your life.

When I raised my frustration in counselling, I recalled, through gritted teeth, the heart-shattering responses to my calls for help. Shrugs and answers like: 'I'm going through my own stuff'; 'If you talk about this, you'll be labelled as fragile and it will ruin your career'; 'Don't talk about this in front of my girlfriend, it'll scare her'; 'I don't know what to say' (literally anything but that). Those comments wore away at my mental health like salt and rust on a mast. Despite the many 'anything I can do' texts I received, when I did ask friends for help, for example asking them to tell people what had happened because I did not have the strength to do it, very few did help me. And because these salt-bearers were external to me, I did not know how to control that variable factor. My therapist was illuminating on the subject:

'I've gotten to a really good place with myself, I think. My yoga training keeps me grounded when the PTSD takes over, I'm getting good at spotting the signs when I start to get overwhelmed and can come back to myself. But I am really, really struggling with some of my friends. I've lost count of how many times I've told them "I need you", and they're just not there. Some haven't even bothered to send one text, in months. When I do see them at a social event, all they do is talk about themselves or moan about their day, and that affects me because I'm an emotional sponge. They don't want to engage with what I'm going through and never ask me how I'm doing. It's all a one-way street and it's breaking my heart, to be honest. I completely understand that they can't be there for me all the time, of course. It's too much for one person. But I'm only one person, and I don't have a choice. I have to go through this every single day, and I feel so alone. How do I make my friends see that I need them?'

'You don't.'

'Then …?'

'You cannot make them see. You have done everything you can to communicate what you need from them. You've made it extremely clear, and they are still refusing to listen, either out of fear or selfishness. Either way, they are unwilling to try to understand what you are going through, because putting themselves in your shoes for even ten seconds is too uncomfortable for them. That is their own choice. It is not your responsibility to change them.'

'Then how do I stay sane while going through this? I can't do this alone.'

'You may think that, but right now they're being bad friends, and that's impacting you. It's changing you, and not for the better. Their bad behaviour is upsetting you, which is completely understandable, but you have enough on your plate right now without that extra layer of pain. It sounds like you have outgrown them, and that happens with friends sometimes. You are taking this challenge head-on and growing as a person. If their vision of life is limited to their own bubble of superficial things, that is their emotional immaturity. You're trying to heal from rape. That is a mammoth task, and you just cannot burden yourself with anything else right now.'

'So what do I do?'

'You cannot change them. So you change the variable you can control – you. You need to distance yourself from these toxic people. Surround yourself only with those who are going to uplift you, or at the very least who on average are going to make you feel good more often than they make you feel low. No one is perfect all the time, they are bound to get it wrong sometimes. But you cannot heal in a toxic environment, and negative people are toxic. You're working so hard to stay positive, so if overall they're undoing your hard efforts and making you feel worse, you must banish them from the sanctity of your personal space.'

'But I work and share friends with some of these people. I can't escape them, so I can't just never speak to them again. It would make things too awkward in the group.'

'You don't have to cut them off. You don't even need to tell them you're doing it. From the sounds of it, some of them are so self-involved they won't even notice anyway. You need to protect yourself, but that doesn't mean fights or even unpleasantness. You need to extract yourself from toxic situations that are draining you and making you unhappy.'

'Right, so in practice, how do I do that?'

'There are two ways. You must create a safe space for yourself by setting boundaries, physical if possible, but mental ones work too. You can physically extract yourself from situations by going out for a walk, taking a break in your car, finding a room with a door you can close or even just putting on headphones. Find somewhere you can be alone and come back to yourself. Limit your contact with these people – don't ring or text them anymore, or at least not as frequently. Sometimes all you might need is a quick time-out to recharge. If you're with them at lunch and they're in that narcissistic mode or complaining about stupid things, for example, get up and go order some coffees.

'Where that's not possible, say you're stuck with them in work or on a trip, you can visualise putting up mental walls to shield yourself. What works well is imagining you're wearing a cloak, and every time they say something judgemental or negative, you visualise those comments bouncing off that cloak. Nothing can touch you. Another example is to imagine your headspace as surrounded by four walls. If someone is sound, they can come in, but if they are going to behave badly or suck all your energy and positivity, they stay out. You control the access to yourself.'

I stared at her, dumbfounded. So beautifully simple. Maybe too simple?

'You can also be proactive about who you do want to see. Ring up the friends who make you feel good, arrange regular coffees or walks with them, keep meeting up with them. You said you were super close to your family, for example. Are you going home and spending time with them?'

'The problem is my family is on the opposite side of that spectrum. They are so supportive and amazing, but it gets almost too intense at times. They keep forgetting and touch my shoulder, try to hold my hand, or come up behind me to hug me when I'm cooking. It triggers me every time. They don't get my reaction because I haven't told them about the violation, but I've withdrawn completely as a result. It's too much to be on edge all the time. I used to be so tactile, they're upset that I can't be affectionate anymore and that makes me feel like a failure, because I'm doing the best I can to get back to normal, and it's still not enough. And yet they are some of the only ones that are unconditionally there for me. I don't know how to control them.'

'It's exactly the same, you don't. You communicate your boundaries to them, and each time they cross them, even if unintentionally, you extract yourself. Go to your room and close the door, take yourself out for a walk. That is your form of taking back control, and you have a lot more of it than you think. It will send a clear reminder, both to you and them, that there are very firm boundaries that must be respected.'

I'm not often stunned into silence, but that did it. Those words were pivotal for me. Suddenly I was aware of the salt and the salt-bearers in my day-to-day life, and wherever possible I began removing them by putting in place those physical and mental boundaries. The process was as empowering as it was painful. Letting go hurts, man. You wonder why the people you love could not step up for you when you needed them most. You ask yourself what you did wrong, why they could not be the friend that you were for them, why they refused to help, what was wrong with *you*. That negative cycle of thinking is salt, too, and you must let go of that as well. You do that in the same way as you remove the salt-bearers: you start by acknowledging its toxic impact on you, then you recognise that it is external to you and accept that you cannot change the thought popping into your head, but you can control your attitude towards it. You extract yourself out of situations when things become too much and bring yourself back to you – you go on your mindful walks, you find your tribe that does support you, you prioritise your self-care and self-compassion.

When recovering from trauma, not just sexual assault or rape but any life-altering trauma, you are passing through one the most trying times of your life and you need to focus all of your attention on your healing. Anything that hinders that needs to be cut loose. You must get as much distance as humanly possible between yourself and the salt-bearers. If anyone makes you feel bad at a time like this, you dump them, and you dump them fast. And just because they beat you to it by ghosting you doesn't mean you can't still dump them. It is an internal decision that you make for yourself to cleanse your life. Now granted, I would be what they call an empath, and so I would be much more sensitive to negativity than most. But that's the point. This is about *you*. This is your time to heal, and you must become unapologetic and ruthless about putting that above everything else. It's not selfishness, it's survival. It is going to take every fibre of your being to get through this. And, as impossible as it feels, it can be done, but you are going to need all the help you can get.

Initially, it's scary. I was afraid there would be no one left by the time I was done with removing the salt. I was scared to lose the people I had been closest to for years, but the idea of who I would become if I stayed with them scared me even more. But I had lost sight that I wasn't emptying out my life. By removing the salt, I was making room for better things. I was allowing shoots to grow in their place. It was the biggest spring-clean of my life. I cut loose the toxic acquaintances, the toxic colleagues and the toxic friends. With each acrid layer I shed, I felt lighter and happier. As painful as the losses were, in their place grew other connections and friendships that were much stronger, much deeper and more meaningful.

Of course, no one will ever handle your situation perfectly. Not even you will achieve that. Everyone has their limits, so you don't have to withdraw from someone just because they let you down a few times. That doesn't make them salt-bearers. It's about where they land on your healing scale. When people drag you down more often than they pull you up, that's when you need to put in the boundaries. I bear my lost friends no ill-will. I understand that they did not have the emotional or mental strength to be there for me. But I am much happier for having distanced and protected myself from the salt. Like a hot-air balloon, when you cut the bags of sand that were weighing you down, you will fly to heights you did not know were possible.

Obviously, removing the salt is not on its own sufficient to heal, otherwise we'd all move to live solo on some desert island and be done with it. No, you must also replant in the ash so that your new life can grow from it. That's a lot easier said than done. When you start off, it feels downright impossible. Looking around you at that field of ashes in those first few months that follow the assault, you're not even sure where to begin. How do you go about an impossible task, like eating an elephant? One bite at a time. It's the same with healing from trauma. It is not going to happen overnight, but it can and will happen, if you put the work in.

So, what are we supposed to replant exactly? This is where Roxanne Battle[12] and Jonathan Van Ness[13] come in. These two powerhouses of positivity talk about creating 'pockets of joy' throughout your day as a way to build up resilience in the face of pain and loss. Pockets of joy are little moments of happiness or pleasure, like brightening up your place with flowers, taking a bubble bath, or even just treating yourself to a nice coffee. These pockets of joy act like seeds. Plant those seeds in the ash (and plenty of them), tend to them, and they will begin to grow shoots that over time will blossom into a flowering life. They start off so small that they seem almost insignificant (*how is a cup of coffee going to cure me from rape and attempted murder exactly?*), but if you get into a practice of finding joy in the small things, they will snowball into something much greater. Chances are, after going through trauma like this, whether it's dissociation or just feeling overwhelmed, you might not be feeling quite like yourself. I certainly wasn't. These seeds allow you to be present and mindful in what you are doing, to reconnect with yourself in manageable, bitesize doses.

The key to these seeds of positivity is consistency. Gardens don't grow in a day, or even a month for that matter. When you plant seeds, you have to give them time to grow. You can't go out there digging them up every day to see if they have started sprouting. It is the same with healing. You have to trust the work you have put in and keep tending to them. Regularly setting mindful moments of joy every single day, no matter how small, is like feeding tiny timbers into a small fire – before you know it, the whole thing is blazing. Your healing must become a practice in its own right. Light a

---

12 *Pockets of Joy: Deciding to Be Happy, Choosing to Be Free*, Roxanne Battle (Whitaker House, 2017).
13 *Over the Top, A Raw Journey to Self-love*, Jonathan Van Ness (HarperCollins, 2019).

candle, get some exercise, declutter your room, make your bed, put on that eye cream, stretch for five minutes, name three things you're grateful for, on paper or in your head. When you do this every day, even on the days when you feel like it isn't achieving anything, you are sending a clear message to your subconscious mind that you matter, and that you are taking your healing into your own hands, no matter the pace. I don't care how small it is, just do it. Some days, I would indulge my OCD streak and fold my bed sheets until they were at the most exact perpendicular angle that was humanly possible to achieve. It may sound incredibly frivolous, but it gave me the tiniest of highs to see how geometrically perfect I could make the folds, which, combined with other tiny highs throughout my day, made me feel like I was slowly taking back control over my mood. The small things matter.

There will be days when you don't have the strength to seek out the small pleasures. Some days (weeks), you might need to hide under the covers and just fall apart. Don't beat yourself up about it. Self-compassion and self-indulgence are seeds of positivity, too, so long as they are practised with awareness and intention. Do your best and try again tomorrow. Trust the process, and whatever you do, just keep going.

In her book *Flourishing*,[14] Dr Maureen Gaffney explains that there is a magic ratio for thriving. Initially identified for relationships, but also applicable in the workplace, that ratio is 5:1. How we experience life is a constant balance between positive and negative experiences – a nice daydream, a fight with a friend, a compliment about your outfit, someone skipping the queue ahead of you, scoring on the dancefloor. There is a critical threshold

---

14 *Flourishing – How to achieve a deeper sense of well-being, meaning and purpose – even when facing adversity*, Dr Maureen Gaffney (Penguin, 2011).

of positivity to negativity of 3:1 for humans to function normally, which means for each negative encounter or thought, you need three positive interactions of the same intensity to balance out that negative one. And that's just to stay level. In order to flourish, that ratio jumps up to five positives for every one negative. In other words, if your boss shouts at you, you need five positive experiences of a comparable level to stay in this state of flourishing. So, for example, one nice coffee and pastry ain't gonna balance out a break-up, but the birth of your child will probably obliterate someone swiping the last brownie. But anything that falls below that critical 3:1 ratio puts you in the danger zone. Dr Gaffney explains that we must seek out as many positive experiences throughout our day as we can in order to keep the gauge on our 'positivity tank' high, so that when a negative experience occurs, we have a healthy buffer against the gauge falling too low. Prevention is always better than cure.

You need to find out whatever 'positives' make your soul happy and throw yourself headfirst into those seeds of joy. Cook a wholesome and delicious meal. Cuddle some animals. Put on an outfit that makes you feel great, even if it's just to admire yourself in your bedroom mirror. Bake pastries, something beautiful. Try your hand at painting. Take photos of things that make you happy. Write. Sing. If some people get annoyed by it – congratulations, the salt-bearers are weeding themselves out for you. Two birds, one happy stone. In their own right, these seeds seem too small to make a difference. But begin to build them up and you might notice your entire perspective begins to change as your 'positivity tank' rises.

For me, it started with colourful breakfast bowls. As simple as that. I'm one of those people who loves taking pictures of my food (haters, back off), and a dish of colourful foods always brings me a tiny dose of joy. So I made those bowls almost daily. I made a point of starting my day on that small positive note. I set up an Instagram page for my yoga business and started posting photos of these bowls, of yoga poses, of quotes and of anything else that made me happy. People engaging with me on the page brought me another little boost of joy. Before I knew it, my small following grew to an insanely positive community of like-minded people who also get excited about small things and always have something nice to say. The salt-bearers probably sneered or found something to criticise. I put even more distance between them and me. I chased the uplifters and the enablers.

Now, as healing as these seeds of positivity are, they cannot grow on their own. Once you've cleared the salt and planted in the ash, those seeds need tending. They need watering. They need sunshine, literally. Get outside and go feel the sun on your skin and the breeze in your hair for a minute. Stop and smell the flowers. Go running, go hiking. Seek out the greenery. Nature is so amazingly healing, I can't put words on it (although the Japanese practice of shinrin-yoku, or 'forest-bathing', comes pretty close). Walk barefoot on grass. This is not your hippie yogi fluffiness, it is documented science. The Earth's surface is electrically negatively charged (as opposed to the air above us, which is positively charged), meaning that it emits negative ions and electrons. Research suggests that walking barefoot on the Earth can act as a grounding conductive system for the ions to flow through our feet and may help combat chronic stress, inflammation, pain, poor sleep, and many other common health disorders.[15]

The biggest breakthrough by far in my own healing journey was yoga. From day one after the assault, my training kicked in and I can genuinely say that it was life-saving. In fact, Dr van der Kolk dedicates a whole chap-

---

15 *Earthing: Health Implications of Reconnecting the Human Body to the Earth's Surface Electrons*, Gaétan Chevalier et al. in Journal of Environmental Public Health (2012).

ter to yoga in *The Body Keeps the Score*, and how it allows PTSD survivors to reinhabit their bodies. Countless MRIs, neuroimaging scans and medical research have been conducted into how yoga activates parts of the brain and, over time, transforms them. Now I know what a lot of people immediately think here, 'I'm not flexible enough to do yoga'. The good news is, you don't need to bend yourself into a pretzel or stand on your head to reap the benefits of it. Yoga is about union. It derives from the Sanskrit root *yuj* (योग), which literally translates as 'to join' or 'to unite'. The very essence of yoga is connecting the body, breath, mind and spirit. It's about harmony between all those things.

Yoga practice teaches us to listen to ourselves. To move through the poses with your breath, you first have to become *aware* of your breathing. To be present, you must first realise your mind has been pulling you away into daydreams, thoughts or memories. To surrender into a pose, you must first notice your body is tense. As you move through your practice, no matter how slow or gentle, you begin to create a sense of belonging to your body. After the assault, I remember just kneeling on my yoga mat and feeling the ground beneath my fingers and palms. I would gently push down into it on every exhale and just *feel* the muscles and joints in my arms and shoulders move. That was my practice, for weeks. That is still yoga. I was reclaiming my mind and body back from the dissociation that had hijacked them, limb by limb. Over time, I began to trust myself more. As my body regained its strength, so did my mind. Every time I conquered a new advanced pose, my faith in myself rekindled a little more. I realised that I might just be able to come back from this. I could do anything I set my mind to.

You don't have to do yoga to heal from trauma. As much as I think yoga is for everyone, you have to honour yourself if you don't feel it's right for you right now. Any exercise that focuses on being present with yourself will work. You need to slowly rebuild trust and harmony between your own body and mind before you can reconnect with the outside world again. Pilates, dancing or Tai Chi are other great ones, to name but a few. Release those endorphins, take back your inner space, rebuild your strength. Every small breakthrough is another shoot taking root into the ashes.

In fact, yoga became about a lot more than simply tending to my seeds of joy. I had been teaching for years, and it brought me a lot of joy to see the penny drop in my students' eyes every time we unlocked a new pose together, or every time a stressed-out lawyer fell asleep in my relaxation sessions. I was sharing my love for yoga and connecting with people who might never have tried it otherwise. And yet, I had never launched my yoga business for fear of failure. Well, one thing going through trauma will do for you is make you realise there is very little in life you truly need to fear.

So I did it.

I took the leap of faith and launched the Busy Warrior Yoga in March 2020. And boy did it take off. Within a year, the Instagram page gained thousands of followers. People were joining my Zoom yoga classes from all over the world – London, Egypt, the Comoros, Japan. I ran yoga fund-raisers for the Rape Crisis Centre, 'Black Lives Matter' organisations, GoFundMe pages. A few days after one of these events, on International Women's Day 2020, Europe went into the first COVID-19 lockdown, and none of what I did would have been possible. It felt a lot like fate, if you believe in such things.

* * *

The other critical part of my healing was therapy. I know there can still be a lot of unease and silence around mental health and illnesses, but thankfully we are starting to stamp out that kind of thinking and we're normalising talking openly about counselling. To be honest with you, I think everyone would benefit from getting regular therapy. I can definitely think of a long list of individuals I know for whom it would do a lot of good.

I completely understand the hesitation or reluctance to get professional help, for one because it can feel like a failure. *'I'm not strong enough to do this on my own.'* I get it. But admitting you need help is a strength. It takes courage to confront your emotions and to ask for help.

I'm no medical expert, but on something like deep-rooted trauma and rape, certainly for me, and probably for most people, I believe that counselling is a necessity. You cannot do this alone, and I say that with all the love in the world. You need help, ideally specialised professional help from people who are trained for this precise trauma. The hardest step will always be the first one. There are helplines and organisations like the Rape Crisis Centre in virtually every country. If therapy really isn't for you, many of these organisations also offer self-led or online programmes (referred to in Chapter 4).

I still remember going to the Rape Crisis Centre for my first counselling session. Walking along a busy Leeson Street, I must have checked over my shoulder half-a-dozen times before walking through the door, terrified someone I knew would see me and uncover my dark secret. But once I walked inside, sat across from my therapist and started talking, all that apprehension just melted away. It was a safe space to open up fully, in my own time, with someone who had probably seen it all and would not show pity, would not be shocked, would just listen. She worked with me to enhance my grounding, combat my PTSD and help with the pressure involved in going back into work. She accepted me for who I was, from my jokes as a coping mechanism to my sassiness when dealing with anger, and the work we did over the next few months was as life-saving as it was healing.

* * *

The other great help in tending my seeds of positivity was journaling. It was an incomparable tool to document my progress and put into words how I was feeling. As I was keeping a diary to track everything for the trial, it was easy to add in asides and streams of consciousness where needed. I tried to focus on minutely identifying my emotions and listing things I felt grateful for. Again, might sound trivial, but there really is something to putting it down on paper. In all honesty, I would probably once have scoffed at the idea, but now I understand the invaluable aid it can be.

Another one I would once have rolled my eyes at is affirmations. These are positive statements that you repeat to yourself to reinforce positive thinking. You know how they say you're supposed to talk to plants? It's exactly the same with this. You have to speak to this garden you are grow-ing. (And this is coming from someone who feels incredibly awkward every time she talks to her parasol plant.) But there is solace in saying things out loud. You're having a great time? Say it. That tree is beautiful? Say it. You're proud of how far you have come? SAY IT, QUEENS AND KINGS. Affir-mations may feel odd at first (they did to me), but they work. Words are powerful, and those spoken out loud even more so.

Then there's 'fake it until you make it'. Did you know that you can trick your brain into reducing stress and lifting your mood, just by smiling? I forced myself to smile a lot. Particularly in the difficult times, in the lead-up to the trial, in the rough days in work, at every disappointment and every setback, I would smile. Not for anyone else. I'd smile on my own, in my room, as I cooked, on my yoga mat. Before falling asleep at night. There are studies showing that the face muscles we use to smile, even a fake smile, stimulate the amygdala (the 'alarm' part of our brain mentioned at Chapter 4, and also the processing centre for our emotions), which in turn triggers the dopamine and serotonin neurotransmitters (sometimes also known as the 'happiness' hormones). Take it from the cynical corporate solicitor.

Those are just a few examples of the key seeds of joy that helped me, but there are so many more to explore. I took the approach that as long as it doesn't hurt, why not try it? Pink salt lamps and burning sage anyone? Old Sarah would have rolled her eyes at those (in fairness, she probably still does a little), but do you know what – if it doesn't hurt anyone, who the hell am I to judge? Some things won't work for you personally, but it's almost more about trying something new and what that says about you. It says loud and clear that you are willing to try anything that might help your healing. It's about showing up for yourself and seeking positivity in all things, without expectation. It also says that you have an open and curious mind, that you are fearless about trying new things, and that you're not going to let a little self-consciousness or embarrassment get in the way of your healing. All quite liberating, really.

Do all of these things, plant your seeds of joy in the ashes of your trauma, steer clear of the salt, tend to them with therapy, exercise, mindfulness, and they will bud and burgeon. They will grow so much that you will become your own centre of grounding, the place you can keep coming back to in times of upheaval and uncertainty.

* * *

There is a Japanese art of repairing broken pottery by fusing the pieces back together with gold, and it is called *Kintsugi*. Kintsugi is built on the idea of embracing flaws for all to see because through the gold sealing, the cracks become both the strongest and most beautiful part of the reassembled ceramic. To me, that is the perfect metaphor for your healing. You may think rape or sexual violence is the end of everything. You may think there is nothing left but ash and the broken pieces of your life. But the worst thing that happened to you can become your greatest opportunity. When you show your whole self, cracks and all, to the world for everyone to see, no one can ever use them to hurt you, and you will inspire others to do the same.

Everything is better now. As nightmarish as the attack and the trial were, and I would wish them on no one, now that I have gone through it, I can honestly say that my life is better for it. When you go through a near-death experience, you realise how utterly trivial certain things in life are to which people blindly attach so much importance. The fancy job, the big title, cushy money, Instagram followers, meaningless sex. Sure, money and comfort are nice, but what matters about all those things is feeling fulfilled. If your six-figure job is primarily spent on material things to distract you – the big fancy holiday you spend all year gagging for, designer clothes that give you a buyer's rush to numb how empty you feel, the most expensive anti-ageing products out there because your high-stress job is taking to your face like a bulldozer to a cornfield, expensive takeaways because you're working late again, and overpriced gym classes to keep the weight of the takeaways off, copious amounts of alcohol just to take the edge off – maybe it's time to rethink your priorities in life. Now don't get me wrong, I have Irish blood, I love a good drink. But when you turn to it or any other self-medication as necessary to unwind, as opposed to out of pleasure, it's time for a readjustment.

I always knew it was not a sustainable or happy lifestyle, but it took a brush with death for me to do something about it. After it, I planted each seed with intention, and there is nothing in my life today that I have not actively chosen. I completely recharted what I wanted to spend my time and energy on in life – my family, my physical and mental health, and my sense of purpose – in that order. I cannot have the last without the first two. Everything else is a bonus. A lot of people are not awake to that. In fact, the system we work in is banking on it. They hope to distract you by dangling the next promotion in front of you and just enough money to keep you comfortable. Well, it's time to step out of the comfort zone.

One silver lining after a rape or sexual assault is that your comfort is taken so far away from you, it's barely a pinprick in the horizon. Once you conquer that, there really isn't much you can't do. Quit that rat race job that's been ruining your mental health for years, ditch the toxic friends, go on that adventure that terrifies you, do the things you've always said you would, and you'll start to develop something that feels suspiciously like happiness. I don't mean to make this sound easy because obviously it's not, but I do mean to tell you that it's very possible. It's taken me two years to get here and I'm still figuring a lot of it out. But the point is I'm moving forward, and you can too.

Rape does not define you. Your trauma does not define you. What defines you is how you meet the challenges and ordeals that were handed to you. How you grow from them. How you treat others. What you make of your life. Your hopes, your dreams, your pursuits and actions. That is who you are. You will never be a sexual violence victim. You are a survivor, a fighter and a warrior.

Sometimes trauma like this can set the scene for your greatest flourishing. You did not choose this. It was not fair. It blew you apart. But if you run from this, you will lose the opportunity to turn it into something incredible. Run headfirst into it. God, it's terrifying, I know. But you have already survived, you are still here. And now, you can do this as well. It's true what they say, that you do not know your own strength until you have no other choice. Sometimes life forces you into positions you prayed you'd never find yourself in, and your only way out is through. I want you to know how strong you are, and no matter how long it takes you to climb up that mountain, you can and you will get there. This is not the end. This is the first chapter of the rest of your life, and it will empower you to be the best version of yourself.

To all the survivors out there – I love you.
If people can hate a complete stranger online for no reason, you can be damn sure I can love one.
I love your strength and your vulnerability.
I love the scars that make you unique.
I love you for your courage even on the days where it doesn't roar.
I love your light and your darkness, because it is only through both that you are whole.

SURVIVAL GUIDE: HEALING

There are many inaccurate depictions out there of what recovering from rape or sexual assault looks like. The truth is that every single person is different. Whatever you are going through, this is your journey and you are the best-placed person to know what it is that you need.

If you are going through the darkness that follows the eruption of trauma, I want you to take my hand and listen to me now. You are not alone in your pain. Others have felt it, too. I have felt it, and I want you to know, from the bottom of my healing heart to yours, that this too will pass. You are the queens and kings who have lost your crown, but you will find a way back to it again. You will laugh again and live again. It can be done. Do the work, trust the process, and keep going, warrior.

Put yourself first: recovering from trauma and PTSD is no small feat, so you must be ruthless and unapologetic about your healing. This is your number one priority. Anyone who does not support that, who makes you feel bad about it or calls you selfish, you tell them to take a hike.

Go at your own pace: as unique as trauma is to each individual, so too is healing. Your recovery path will not follow anyone else's. Be patient with yourself and allow yourself to process how you are feeling. You are not going to start healing immediately, and when you do there will be ups and downs. Just keep going, you are on the right track.

Give yourself time to grieve: you may feel like your old life is gone forever. You might also not experience this feeling at all, but if you do, you have to give yourself time to grieve for that life. Acknowledge what you're going through and allow yourself to feel it. That is not to say that your life is over or that you will feel this way forever. But you need to go through this process so that you can move on. Stay kind to yourself during it.

Seek out the small moments of joy: you need to *do* things for yourself to start tackling this monster. You don't have to start big. Do small things that bring you small joy or motivate you, no matter how little. Draw yourself a bath, light a candle, treat yourself to a nice coffee, bake, paint, apply a facial mask. Pack as much self-care as you can into your day, every day. It is said that it takes about thirty days to form a new habit, so set yourself this daily goal for a month and watch it snowball into a deeper sense of positivity.

Cut loose the 'salt-bearers': get as much distance as humanly possible between toxic people and yourself – be they colleagues, friends or even family members. You need to focus on your healing right now, so anyone who is pulling you down, cut contact or distance yourself.

Create a safe space: when you cannot physically avoid some toxic people (e.g. if you live or work with them), you can still set boundaries to protect the sanctity of your headspace. You can extract yourself from situations by taking a time-out in your car, closing the door of your room, or going for a walk. You can also visualise a cloak or four walls around you to not let people get to you – this is your space. If people are draining your energy or positivity, imagine the cloak or walls closing around to shield you. They can come in if they are sound; if not, they stay out. Visualisation is a powerful tool for your mind to take back control.

Surround yourself with people who uplift you: it might surprise you who those people are, but if they make you feel good and accepted, seek out their company as much as possible. And remember, no one will get it right every time. The key is that they make you feel better more often than not.

Open the lines of communication: unless someone has been through trauma like this, it is very difficult for them to understand what you're going through. Don't be afraid to tell people what you need in order to heal. For example, if someone around you is being negative all the time, gently explain how that is impacting your mindset.

Beware of self-medication: I'm the last person to judge here or tell you what not to do, I'm half-Irish so I like my drink (especially my wine, being half-French and all). The only thing I'll say is trauma of this magnitude is an Everest to conquer, and it's a slippery slope if you fall. You don't have to go abstinent on the cocktails, but equally try to watch out for excessive self-medicating, not just alcohol but drugs or other substances too. You want to safeguard your physical and mental health as much as you can. And give yourself a break if you cave occasionally. Balance in everything.

Try yoga or Pilates: after a rape or sexual assault, it's important to reconnect and rebuild love and trust with your body. Ideally, start with something gentle and mindful and that you can practice in a safe space, like yoga or Tai Chi.

Exercise: you're gonna roll your eyes at me, but exercise is crucial. I know, I know, but self-care ain't all about facials and treats, sometimes you need to do things that you don't want to do in the moment but that will benefit you long-term. As you regain your strength, build back up to something you enjoy, like running, swimming, dancing or Calisthenics. Get those endorphins pumping because they are nature's best remedy.

Get into nature: go wherever you instinctively gravitate to – mountains, the seaside, rivers or forests. Personally, I find the colour green extremely healing (and, depending on where you live, parks can be easier to come by than beaches). Make a point of getting out and feeling the fresh air on your face or feasting your eyes on the scenery.

Practice gratitude: if you don't know how to do this, start by just looking around you and finding three things you are grateful for right now. I don't care how small – that sun ray coming in through the window, the existence of coffee, birdsong, nachos. Do it frequently, and your perspective may start to shift and become generally more positive.

Journal: if you're not comfortable with journaling (I wasn't), try lists, bullet-points, or one-liners. It is important to keep a record to be able to acknowledge your progress, especially on the bad days, and also if you're to give evidence in trial (see Chapter 8). You can also use it as a two-in-one to practice recording your gratitude too.

Join a choir, even if you can't sing: trust me, I can't sing, but singing in a group has been proven to release endorphins and helps you synchronise with other people. Particularly if you're struggling with social interactions or being close to people, this is a great way to slowly reintroduce yourself back into society and build up a feeling of connection and belonging.

Make yourself smile: I forced myself to smile, especially on the bad days. It may sound silly, but I was impressed by how much it worked. It has been well-documented that smiling, even a fake smile, stimulates the brain chemicals related to positivity (dopamine and serotonin).

Get therapy: this is another crucial one. Think of it like a deep cut that requires stitches. If you don't seek professional care, you might bleed to death or it might get infected, and for sure it will leave a nasty scar. It is not weak to seek help, it is a sign of intelligence and strength. If you really can't bring yourself to do it, at the very least speak honestly to a friend. You need to let it out, or your bottled-up feelings will solidify and become very hard to shift. If therapy is not for you, check out Chapter 4's checklist for some self-led professional programmes.

Disclosure of counselling records: I have covered this in Chapter 4, but it bears repeating because it's something you really need to know in advance. In Ireland, your therapy notes can be used as evidence in court. If you are worried about this, you can discuss the note-taking with your therapist. Check out the Survival Guide at the end of Chapter 4 for full details on this – fight fire with fire.

EPILOGUE:

Free

Forgiveness is the last bolt in the machine that will set you free. It is the final step in truly letting go. There can be no moving on from this place without it. You can choose to put what happened to you in a box and never deal with it, but you will leave a piece of yourself behind in that process, and you will never be whole as you move forward. The fiery demons of anger and resentment will always haunt your shadow.

The act of forgiving goes beyond just letting go, it requires embracing an understanding of, and even a compassion for, the people who hurt you. That goes not just for your abuser, but for all the salt-bearers, too: the friends, family members, colleagues and institutions who let you down. It goes for forgiving yourself as well. Healing is no easy task, and chances are that in that process you will not have been kind to yourself all of the time. We allowed ourselves to feel great shame or guilt even though it was not our fault, we withdrew from life and friends, we pushed ourselves too hard, we asked ourselves what is wrong with *us*.

I speak from a place of great humility here, because I am well aware that as horrific as my story was, I was one of the lucky ones. I was believed. My case made it to trial. I had training in mindfulness and mental resilience. I knew the law and could stand up for myself. I had family support to do it for me when I wasn't able to do it. I didn't know my attacker. What happened to me was a senseless act, committed by a lost soul. He was and is a complete stranger to me. I will never have to see him again. I will never have to face his friends, his family or anyone else who knows him. My parents will never run into his parents at the local shop. I will never have to experience the fear of seeing him while out on the town. For the majority of survivors, that is not the case. Most incidents of rape and sexual assault happen with someone known to you, your boss, a family member, a friend or a date.

My journey, which came damn close to breaking me, was by far one of the easier ones. I still feel rage knowing that there are heroes out there who have to live with the reminder of what happened to them every day, who are not free to speak about what they have endured, and who have to go on about their life carrying this impossible weight. I cannot begin to fathom the strength that takes. I am so humbled by your courage and full of admiration for you.

And yet, I truly believe that forgiveness is the ultimate step in your healing process. It is the hardest thing you will ever have to do, but it is transformational.

There is an ancient Hawaiian tradition of reconciliation and forgiveness called Ho'Oponopono, which loosely translates as 'restoring equilibrium' or 'putting back to right'. The rite is often expressed through the Ho'Oponopono prayer, which turns on four statements: *I'm sorry. Please forgive me. Thank you. I love you.* Often performed to reconcile conflicts in families or communities, the prayer is practiced by holding someone who wronged you in your mind and repeating this mantra slowly, with intention. Beautifully simple, the ritual combines four formidably powerful forces – repentance, atonement, gratitude and love.

The Hawaiians understood very early that holding on to hurt can attract disease. That's something that Western medicine has only caught up to much more recently (see Chapter 5 for a recap on the physical harms of anger). This prayer is cleansing because it starts with yourself. Think of any time you have put yourself in harm's way, be it a small, damaging thought or a self-destructive pattern. Repeat the mantra. After a few minutes, move on to other people. Think of the small hurts and the big betrayals. Repeat the mantra. It is hard. It is not like waving a magic wand and *poof*, everyone is forgiven. It takes time, but it is miraculous. I've said it before and I'll say it again – words are incredibly powerful.

The first mantra of the prayer can be misleading. It does not mean *I'm sorry* in an apologetic sense, but instead expresses that we feel sorry about the situation at hand. It is a human need that others acknowledge how we feel, but by saying *I'm sorry* we are taking ownership of that acknowledgement on ourselves. We recognise that the wrong exists and we are respecting our feelings by holding space for them. Like anger, we must feel the hurt before letting it go. If we dodge or push our feelings away, they will only bubble back stronger.

The second mantra, *Please forgive me,* shows self-compassion (but not regret) for having let ourselves be hurt by a situation. It also adds to collective forgiveness – where we are not be able to forgive, we ask for forgiveness for wrongs we have done instead. As we forgive, so too are we forgiven. This second mantra shows us the aspects we are stuck on, what is preventing us from moving on, and often draws internal questions to the surface: *why do*

I need to be forgiven? What did I do wrong? Let these questions come to you without immediately seeking to answer them. The answers will follow over time.

The third mantra, *Thank you*, infuses great positivity into a negative situation. No matter what the hurt was, there will always be some silver lining to it. Maybe we learnt something from this, maybe we became more resilient because of it or can help someone else as a result. In exactly the same manner as the practice of gratitude, this mantra allows us to reshape our perspective by getting into a discipline of seeking out the good everywhere we look.

The fourth, *I love you*, is the most difficult one of all, but this is where the magic happens. In this final step, we go beyond simply letting go, and we embrace total acceptance of our journey. We cleanse our souls of the salt and all that is toxic. Choosing love over hate is the will of the strong. It is the most powerful act a person can commit in their life.

The wounded ego will greatly resist this prayer because we have been taught to resent those who hurt us. The greater the hurt, the stronger the resistance. We have been taught that justice involves seeking out and punishing the guilty. Showing repentance by saying *Please forgive me* for something that was not your fault feels inherently unfair and, as my friends know, I am not one to roll over and take things lying down. Initially, I found it very difficult to accept. As I said the words, my deep-rooted sense of justice felt outrage at the self-sacrifice. It took time for me to understand that that sense of justice and feistiness all boiled down to ego. Not in the narcissistic sense, but in the individualistic meaning of the term. I had allowed myself to look at things around me through my eyes only.

Ego has been central to the development of our justice system, our ethics and morals, even our society. We seek to regulate others' actions to ensure the group is duty-bound to protect the individual. It all turns on, what do others owe *me*? But Ho'Oponopono is about acknowledging that everything we experience in life is our own personal responsibility. It's about recognising that you have a choice. We choose how we react to the cards handed to us. While you cannot control external things or people's actions, what is under your remit is your internal perception of these things: every thought you have and every emotion you feel about them makes up your reality. That goes for war, betrayals, famine, rape, ghosting, all of it.

The reason this practice spoke to me so much was because it is so empowering. The Ho'Oponopono prayer allows you to take responsibility without creating guilt. You can choose to stop reliving the hurt inflicted and let it go. It does not mean erasing the wrong or not wishing it had never happened. It means turning a negative into a greater good and restoring harmony. You alone control your internal peace. That is, of course, far easier said than done, like all things to do with healing of this magnitude, but it *is* within your power. You just need to learn how to exercise it, and you do that through practice and repetition.

Each time I repeated those words, I felt a tiny ounce of weight lift off my chest. That's the thing about forgiveness, it draws anger from your body like sucking poison out of a snake bite. Sometimes I had to say them out loud to force my ego to listen.

Initially, I practised Ho'Oponopono for me, to free myself from the heavy weight of resentment. But as I began embracing the words, I had to pass through the process of practising it for the salt-bearers as well. Over time, I came to feel some empathy for those I was forgiving. I accepted their limitations, their pain and their perspective. That is not to say I absolved their sins or condoned their actions, but I did come to realise that we may not be as far apart from each other as I thought. I felt a warmth in my core, something was changing inside of *me*. I was the sculptor reshaping the damaged clay by smoothing it over and over with mindfulness and intention.

* * *

I thought I had forgiven. I told myself that I forgave Beast a long time ago, but then the raging fires of anger sneaked up on me. I allowed myself to forget that forgiveness is never static. Despite having 'forgiven' him, I continued to call him Beast, convincing myself that I was simply not able to speak his name. As we approached trial, at every trigger, fury would raise its scaly head again. To me he would always be Beast because the only time I came into contact with him, that is what he was. But that does not make the person he is deep down a beast.

Forgiveness is a journey. It is something you must practice daily, that is why it is transformational. Forgiveness is a choice I will make every day for the rest of my life. I am still learning, and it is still something I get wrong on some days. But as painful as what I went through was, I am a better person for it today. Something as life-shattering as rape or sexual violence will be one of your greatest challenges, but it is also an opportunity to transform. It took me breaking into a million pieces to realise that I needed to crack open for the light to enter me.

Ultimately, it's about not letting this define you. You are sacred, and you do not have to let this alter you for the worse. You have a choice. You can be angry, or you can choose forgiveness. You can choose to be ruled by fear and resentment, or by love and compassion. You will always have that choice, no one can take it away from you. And it is through that choice that you define your entire life. It is what you make of it. You have lost nothing. You have been robbed of nothing. You have been given the opportunity to rise to a version of yourself that you could only have previously dreamed of.

The girl I am leaving behind, I have hugged her a hundred times in my mind and yet I have never been completely ready to let her go, until now. I am sending her off with nothing but love, and I am choosing to close that chapter of my life, for good. Ashes to ashes. I am finally free to turn my focus towards this new beginning.

Maybe that's what was holding me back all this time. For so long, I was angry because I did not feel listened to. All I wanted was to connect with others, and instead there was only emptiness and silence. But the tidal wave of support I was met with after going public had me on a high for weeks. Just with love.

Maybe the salt-bearers are toxic because they feel unloved, too. Maybe my friends stayed away because facing their fear and limitations was just too painful for them. Maybe the colleagues and people I looked up to who let me down felt guilt for not being able to step up to the mark. Maybe the criminal justice practitioners are jaded because they have lost sight of the main objective of the justice system. Maybe Beast never had someone to stick up for him or teach him any better.

To the salt-bearers who were in pain from all the salt they were carrying and did not know how to put down, I forgive you. The lost friends who were even more terrified than I was, I forgive you. The people and colleagues who failed me because they couldn't face how much bigger than them this was, I forgive you. The taciturn doctor and the bitter receptionist who lashed out from their own pent-up anger, I forgive you. The criminal justice practitioners who lost a piece of themselves along the way, I forgive you. Ibrahim, I forgive you.

I'm sorry. Please forgive me. Thank you. I love you.

ACKNOWLEDGEMENTS

Books take a long time in the making, but this story is the meshing of formidable forces who all rose to the occasion. I am humbled by the riptide of love and emotional support every one of you sent my way, from the wake of the assault until now. This book is as much yours as it is mine.

To Alison, my partner in crime, teacher, confidant, at times therapist and all-time best friend. I won the lottery with you as my sister. Thank you for always having my back, for tirelessly reading draft after draft and listening to my endless brainstorming on this book, for making me laugh even on the dark days, for your selfless strength and bulletproof loyalty. There is no greater love in my life than you.

To my parents, my pillars in any storm, you both taught me love, empathy and strength in your different ways. I am only who I am today because of you. *À Maman*, who raised us to see the good in all things, great and small, for teaching me long before any of this happened to always be kind to others because you never know what someone is going through. To Dad, who never encountered a problem he couldn't solve, for always being there and showing me that bravery is not always a blazing fire, sometimes it's the flickering flame that refuses to die out.

To Erika, Kunak and Eileen, the three legendary Irish heroines who stepped up even when I was pushing everyone away, thank you for never letting me forget what kickass women can achieve. To the McGann and Grace clans for always standing by my side and cheering me on.

I will never be able to thank the Dublin Rape Crisis Centre and the

Sexual Assault Treatment Unit enough for the relentless, life-saving, stigma-shattering work they do every day. You launched me on this course of healing and personal growth, my trajectory would have been very different were it not for you incredible women and men.

My thanks to Una Mullally, friend and champion of women, who gave me and so many others a voice when no one else was listening. You were the conduit that brought my story to light, and your beautifully crafted words set me free.

The amazing O'Brien Press team who honoured me by asking me to write this book, and without who none of this would have been possible. Thank you for believing in me. To Michael O'Brien and Kunak McGann, for your guidance and vision from day one. To my editor, Rachel Pierce, for your eagerness, patience and, above all, for never letting the fact that I was a complete amateur author get in the way of anything.

To my colleagues and mentors who reached out in a personal capacity to extend goodwill and encouragement. I carry your words with me every day. Special thanks to friend and role-model Davinia Conlan. Your kindness, support and serenity were the flicker of light I needed to believe in myself again.

To my sensational friends who rallied in my darkest hour and who each walked some of this path with me, if I could name you all, I would. Thank you for your unwavering faith in me that I could achieve this when I thought I couldn't, and your words from the heart that made me cry.

In particular, for your outstanding contribution to this book – reading drafts, talking ideas through, offering designs and holding my hand as I progressively lost my mind during the writing process – thank you Nikki Conway, Clara Gleeson, Lynn Lambe, Paul Fitzpatrick, Paul Feeney, and

Ben Studer. I am standing on your shoulders today.

My yoga students and the Busy Warrior Yoga community, you were the place of healing I needed, body and soul. Every day you inspire me through your talent, creativity, humour and light.

To the survivors and their loved ones who shared your stories of battles and bravery with me. To every single one of you who picked up this book because you want to make a difference, particularly you amazing men who care more about creating a safer world for women than being judged for speaking up.

You are all my heroes.

Great books from

Hundreds of books
for all occasions

From beautiful gifts to books you won't want to be parted from! Great writing, beautiful illustration and leading design. Discover books for readers of all ages.

Follow us for all the latest news and information, or go to our website to explore our full range of titles.

 TheOBrienPress  TheOBrienPress

 OBrienPress  TheOBrienPress

Visit, explore, buy
obrien.ie